A Bridge to God

A Little Book with Big Insights

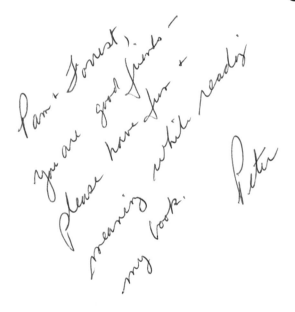

The Rev. Peter K. Stimpson

ISBN 978-1-64416-479-2 (paperback)
ISBN 978-1-64416-480-8 (digital)

Christian Faith Publishing, Inc.
832 Park Avenue
Meadville, PA 16335
www.christianfaithpublishing.com

Printed in the United States of America

To my wife, Lauren, whose love and support I treasure.

Contents

Preface

Why Did I Write This Book?

My name is Peter Stimpson. I am a priest and therapist, and I have written this book as a gift from me to you. It holds my reflections on the major questions that we all ask. Does God exist? Is Jesus Christ the Son of God? What is the purpose of life? Why does God allow suffering? Why do bad things happen to good people? Is there life after death?

I have spent my life exploring these issues, and have revealed what I have learned when preaching at various churches in the states of New York, New Jersey, and Virginia. Knowing that is a fairly limited audience, and knowing that everyone wants answers to these questions, I decided to write this book.

Let me tell you a story. While my ministry was largely as a Director of counseling services, I also offered my help to poor churches in need of a priest. From 1983–1988, I was helping All Saints' Episcopal Church in Round Lake, New York, just a half-hour's drive north of Albany. The bishop sent me there to close the church, as there were only six to ten attending services, and the building was in desperate need of major repairs. I was not much on closing churches, so I convinced the bishop to let me try and save it. The parishioners and I worked hard, and over the five years I was there, we got the numbers up to sixty on Sundays, renovated the church, built a hall, and put enough in the bank to hire a half-time priest to take my place.

During those years, I met a man who was a chemist. His wife came to church, but he was a professed atheist. He was a mountain climber, and understandably found his meaning from the beauty and majesty of nature. He and I liked each other, and we had many a long conversation about God and the meaning of life. Gradually, he began to come to church, and our talks continued and deepened.

Then one day, he told me that he had developed cancer, probably due to his exposure to chemicals over his career. He was diagnosed in May and died a few months later at the end of the summer. I loved him, and so his death was a hard loss for me, as well as for his family. After his death, his wife went through his things, one of which was his wallet. Stuffed inside was an old piece of paper that was folded over many times so as to fit. It was a poem about a climber, and one that touched me so deeply that I have used it ever since at funerals. It was noted as being anonymous, but many years later, I discovered it was written by Will Allen Dromgoole in 1900. Here it is.

We Will Never Again Pass this Way

An old man going a lone highway,
Came at the evening, cold and gray,
To a chasm, vast and deep and wide,
Through which was flowing a sullen tide.
The old man crossed in the twilight dim,
The sullen stream has no fears for him,
But he turned when safe on the other side,
And built a bridge to span the tide.
"Old Man," said a fellow pilgrim near,
"You are wasting your time with building here;
You never again will pass this way,
Your journey will end with the closing day.
You have crossed the chasm, deep and wide,
Why build you this bridge at evening tide?"
The Builder lifted his old gray head;
"Good Friend, in the way I've come," he said,
"There followed after me today
A Youth whose feet must pass this way,
This stream that has been as naught to me,
To the fair-haired Youth might a pitfall be.
He, too, must cross in the twilight dim,
Good Friend, I am building the bridge for him."

This book is my bridge that I built for you. It is not meant to be a theological tome, but rather the reflections of a priest on life. Read it in that light, and if it helps you in your life's journey, then I am happy.

I do not taut myself as some quintessential guru, sitting atop a mountain handing out pearls of wisdom, but instead a man whose has had to face life like anyone else. I have had to wrestle with pain, suffering, and doubt, and have journeyed through philosophy, theology, and psychology to find answers that would carry me over the chasm of doubt to peace and meaning. Now, fellow sojourner, let me give you my bridge.

1
Does God Exist?

Why the Search?

When I was fourteen, my father died. He had been sick with cancer for three years, his illness taking him from a robust man of two hundred twenty-five pounds down to a skeleton of eighty-nine pounds.

When my brother came into the living room to tell me that Dad had died, I went next door to the Catholic Church to pray. I went to church daily, and I wanted to try to make sense of the senseless. But I left more confused than I entered, and my faith, which was understandably weak and immature, wavered under the weight of the death of my father.

I began to wonder how there could be a God who would allow such suffering and death. I would not say that I became an atheist, but I probably was an agnostic. And yet, I knew that answering the question of whether God existed was of the greatest importance. If he did, then I wanted to spend my life in his service. If he did not, then I would pursue a different path.

After high school, I chose to enter the seminary, both because I always felt a calling to be a priest, and because I realized that if I wanted to find an answer to my question, what better place than a seminary. I entered Mater Christi Seminary in Albany, New York, in 1964. It was a Roman Catholic minor seminary, which in 1966 was followed by six years in a major seminary, St. Paul's Seminary in Ottawa, Canada. The first four years of the eight years of seminary were spent studying philosophy. Most seminarians hated philosophy, wanting to get to the last four years that would be devoted to the study of theology. But as philosophy literally means the love of wisdom, giving you proofs rather than faith, it was perfect for me. I could not get enough.

While the study of philosophy is a much broader field than looking at the existence of God, nonetheless, I treasured the opportunity of looking over the centuries of humanity searching for the same answer as me. Many of the proofs for the existence of God seemed to have flaws in them, such as René Descartes's famous statement, "Cogito ergo sum" (I think, therefore, I am), his premise being that if you think of God, he must exist. But I can think of unicorns and a lot of things that do not exist, so my search continued.

What follows is the proof upon which I settled, being a take on one of the proofs of Thomas Aquinas, a twelfth century monk and theologian, whose basic work, *Summa Theologica*, jumped off the page at me.[1]

The Proof

Imagine a circle within which everything exists: you, me, rocks, trees, animals, fish, houses, buildings of all sorts, and so forth. What do they all have in common?

The answer is that nothing can create itself. You and I are the results of our mothers becoming pregnant, as are animals. Our homes were constructed by artisans. Trees result from seeds dropped from other trees. And so forth.

Well, if nothing inside the circle can create itself, from where did the circle come? The answer is that we must posit that there is one being outside the circle who creates at least one being inside the circle, and we call that being outside the circle "God."

I have come to see the validity of evolution over my lifetime, science making such a strong case that it really cannot be denied. But that only tells us how creation occurred, still leaving the question of how it began.

---

[1]   Pegis, Anton C., Ed., *Basic Writings of Saint Thomas Aquinas,* vol. 1 (New York: Random House, 1945), 18–24.

Challenge to the Proof

Some have challenged the above proof by the theory of the conservation of energy, namely, that while energy may take different forms over time, the amount of energy remains the same. It has always been there.

But what are the formulas for energy? Potential energy is defined as weight times height. Imagine a boulder at the top of a cliff.

If you push the boulder off the cliff, it has kinetic energy, which is defined as one-half the mass times the velocity squared. If you are unlucky enough to be under the boulder when it lands, you are squished.

How does that help defend my proof? Well, the point is that you cannot define energy without matter, that is, the boulder. So, from where did the boulder come? Therefore, you are right back to the crux of my proof.

Defense from Scientists

In recent years, I have been enthralled to learn of how scientists are coming to posit the existence of a creator. An example would be Francis S. Collins, who wrote a fascinating book, *The Language of God: A Scientist Presents Evidence for Belief.* He was an atheist who became a believer based upon scientific research. He was the leader of the international Human Genome Project that revealed the DNA sequence, showing us how we developed as humans, which in his mind revealed "the language of God."

When considering creation, he notes,

> The existence of the Big Bang begs the question of what came before that, and who or what was responsible. It certainly demonstrates the limits of science as no other phenomenon has done. The consequences of Big Bang theory for theology are profound. For faith traditions that describe the universe as having been created by God from nothingness (ex nihilo), this is an electrifying outcome.

He adds, "The Big Bang cries out for a divine explanation. It forces the conclusion that nature had a defined beginning. I cannot see how nature could have created itself. Only a supernatural force that is outside of space and time could have done that."[2]

Later in his book, reflecting upon the complexity of his own research into the human genome, Dr. Collins noted, "Despite massive improbabilities, the properties of the universe appear to have been precisely tuned for life," pointing again in his mind to the existence of an intelligent, spiritual being at the beginning of time.[3]

How interesting that science has become an ally of theology, but then again, truth is one. Science is not to be feared, but embraced. Science does help us to understand the creator when looking at the beginning of, and then the complexity of, life.

Attributes of God

Okay, so God exists. But what more can be said about God?

Well, if God created out of nothing, if God has control over the natural, then God is above nature, that is, supernatural. And if supernatural, then God is neither limited by natural laws, nor by time. God must be omnipresent (not limited by place), eternal (not limited by time), omnipotent (not limited in power), and omniscient (not limited in knowledge).

This is not only very interesting but also tantalizing, leaving us yearning for so much more. The answer to our next question will give us more, a lot more.

---

[2] Collins, Francis S., *The Language of God: A Scientist Presents Evidence for Belief* (New York: Free Press, 2006), 56.
[3] Collins, page 145.

2

Is Jesus Christ the Son of God?

Faith

When I entered the second four-year period of seminary, the focus was squarely upon theology, the study of God. However, unlike philosophy, theology was based upon faith.

What is faith? It is not a whimsical belief in something that is improbable, like the Easter Bunny or the tooth fairy. Faith is defined as an ascent of the intellect. Our mind must make the jump from what we can prove to what we need to believe. But it is based on thinking, not misguided feelings.

Obviously, Christianity is based upon the belief that Jesus Christ is the Son of God? Is he?

The Prophecies

Well, to understand who Jesus Christ is, let us first look at the prophecies in the Old Testament that predicted his coming, that is, the coming of the Messiah.

The whole idea of the need for a Messiah was based upon the premise that since the fall, the "original" sin of Adam and Eve, that God would send someone to "deliver" mankind from the mess that had developed over centuries, returning mankind to a renewed covenant with God.

But please realize that the Bible is a process of increasingly understanding God and his relationship with us. For instance, our understanding of God evolves, such as from an angry God who tells the Prophet Samuel to instruct King Saul to kill every man, woman, and child when attacking the Amalekites (1 Samuel 15:18) to Jesus telling a shocked crowd that we should love our enemies (Matthew 5:43–48).

In the same way, the understanding of the Messiah evolved, from a warrior king who would lead the armies of Israel to free them from the powers of the time (Assyria, Babylon, Persia, Greece, or Rome), to a suffering servant whose death would free his people from the stranglehold of sin. He would be anointed by God, the word for anointed being Messiah, which translated into Greek becomes Christos, and in English, "Christ."

Nonetheless, the interesting thing about the prophecies is that they are all fulfilled in the person of Jesus of Nazareth. Here are four of these prophecies:

1. *The Messiah will be Born in the Lineage of King David*
    Nathan was a prophet under King David (1000–961 BC) who told David that his kingdom would endure forever (2 Samuel 7:16; Psalm 89:12), the assumption then being that the Messiah would be a king in his lineage. Joseph, the husband of Mary, was in the lineage of King David, this being the reason he had to return to Bethlehem to be counted during the census of Caesar Augustus, as Bethlehem was the town in which David was born, and all people had to return to the town of their birth.

2. *The Messiah will be Born in Bethlehem*
    As the Messiah was to come in the lineage of King David, it made sense that he would be born in the town where David was born, Bethlehem. This then became the prophecy of Micah (750–687 BC), who said "But you, Bethlehem Ephrathah, though you are small among the clans of Judah, out of you will come for me one who will rule over Israel, whose origins are from of old, from ancient times" (Micah 5:2). Again, as noted above, Joseph had to return to Bethlehem for the census, and there Jesus was born in a manger.

3. *The Messiah will be born of a virgin and called Emmanuel*

The first hint of the divinity of the Messiah comes from the prophet Isaiah (742–701 BC). Isaiah had been summoned by Ahaz, King of Judah (735–715 BC), for advice when Jerusalem was besieged by King Rezin of Damascus and King Pekah of the northern kingdom of Israel, they hoping to force Ahaz to join them in a foolhardy rebellion against the major power of the day, Assyria.

While others advised sending a messenger for help to Assyria, Isaiah told Ahaz to put his trust in God, giving him a sign of God's love and support, namely, that the Messiah would be born of a virgin and that his name would be Emmanuel, the translation of which is "God is with us" (Isaiah 7:14).

This prophecy was rejected, seeming utterly crazy and useless, but was so wild that it was always remembered. It would not dawn on people for hundreds of years that if the Messiah were to be both God and man, he could not be born of a human father and that, therefore, the mother would have to be a virgin.

Jesus was born of Mary, who was pregnant, but not by Joseph, he having debated to "divorce her quietly" until he was told in a dream that "what is conceived in her is from the Holy Spirit" (Matthew 1:18–21).

Mary had learned of the divine origin of her pregnancy from the Angel Gabriel, telling her when she inquired, "How can this be, since I am a virgin" that "The Holy Spirit will come upon you, and the power of the Most High will overshadow you" (Luke 1:26–37).

4. *The Messiah will be "A Suffering Servant"*

Many years later, another person who belonged to an Isaian school of religious thought and whose words thus became part of the book of Isaiah, wrote a prophecy of the Messiah that was quite different than a conquering king. The author was called Deutero-Isaiah, or "Second Isaiah," and lived after the kingdom of Judah had been conquered by the Babylonians (587 BC), the discouraged and downtrodden Judeans being exiled to Babylon, where this author then wrote to bring hope and encouragement to the Jews.

As the kingdom of Judah no longer existed, the Messiah would no longer be a king but now was seen as "a suffering servant," who, by living a life and enduring suffering without sinning would break the chain of sin from Adam to the present. The suffering servant is one who "offered my back to those who beat me, my cheeks to those who pulled out my beard; I did not hide my face from mocking and spitting" (Isaiah 50:6). His actions have a salvific purpose, Isaiah noting, "he was pierced for our transgressions, he was crushed for our iniquities; the punishment that brought us peace was upon him, and by his wounds we are healed" (Isaiah 53:5). And even the manner of the servant's death foretells the suffering of Jesus, "He was oppressed and afflicted, yet he did not open his mouth; he was led like a lamb to the slaughter, and as a sheep before her shearers is silent, so he did not open his mouth" (Isaiah 53:7).

Jesus, indeed, suffered. He was mocked by the Sanhedrin, by Herod Antipas, by the soldiers who slapped his face and pressed a crown of thorns upon his head, and tortured by other soldiers who scourged him at the pillar, and eventually crucified him. As Paul tells us in his Epistle to the Hebrews, unlike the high priests who annually offered the sacrifice of an animal to atone for the sins of the people on Yom Kippur, Jesus, being God, had only to offer it once for all people of all times. "Day after day every priest stands and performs his religious duties; again and again he offers the same sacrifice, which can never take away sins. But when this priest (Jesus) had offered for all time one sacrifice for sins, he sat down at the right hand of God" (Hebrews 10:11–14).

The Miracles

The prophecies that Jesus fulfilled help us to see him as the Messiah, but the issue is whether he was God.

Miracles are a big step toward understanding that Jesus was divine. The lame walked, the blind saw, the deaf heard, the mute spoke, the sick returned to health, and those who died returned to life.

Not bad! Can you do that? No. Well, who could? How about the Son of God?

Miracles are not common in our age. Why? Well, they have a purpose. They are not primarily for the person affected, but for the crowd to understand something. In the case of Jesus, they affirmed his claim to be the Son of God. In the case of the apostles, they pointed to the power of God granted them through their relationship with Jesus.

As apostles are also credited with having performed miracles, one can claim that the divinity of Jesus cannot rest solely upon the miracles. However, remember that the apostles invoked the name of Jesus when performing miracles whereas Jesus spoke only to his Father. And the sheer number of his miracles, not only over people but also over nature, made the apostles marvel that he must, indeed, be God.

Here is a list of some of the miracles. While a partial list, the complete list can be found in the Life Application Study Bible, NIV New International Version, page 1797.

Miracles of Nature	Matthew	Mark	Luke	John
Turning Water into Wine				2:1–11
Feeding 5,000	14:15–21	6:35–44	9:12–17	6:5–14
Calming the Storm	8:23–27	4:35–41	8:22–25	
Walking on Water	14:22–33	6:45–52		6:17–21
Multiplying Fish			5:1–11	21:1–14

Miracles of Persons	Matthew	Mark	Luke	John
A Paralytic	9:1–8	2:1–12	5:17–26	
A Lame Man				5:1–16
A Leper	8:1–4	1:40–45	5:12–15	

Miracles of Persons	Matthew	Mark	Luke	John
Ten Lepers			17:11–19	
Peter's Mother-in-Law	8:14–17	1:29–31	4:38–39	
Blind Bartimaeus	20:29–34	10:46–52	18:35–43	
Man Born Blind				9:1–7
Two Blind Men	9:27–31			
Blind Man at Bethsaida		8:22–26		
Centurion's Servant	8:5–13		7:1–10	
Official's Son at Cana				4:46–54

Miracles of Persons				
Jairus's Daughter	9:18–26	5:22–43	8:41–56	
Widow's Son			7:11–16	
Lazarus				11:1–45

Skepticism

Even in the face of such evidence, some people doubt the veracity of the miracles. To dispel doubt, let us look at two of the miracles.

Jesus walking on water. Some question the miracle of Jesus walking on water by claiming that he must have been walking along the shore, that is, not very deep in water, and so it gave the appearance to the apostles that he was walking on top of the water.

But let us look at what the scriptures say. The Gospel of Matthew notes that the boat holding the apostles "was already at a considerable distance from land"; the Greek translation is "many stadia" (Matthew 14:24). One stadion was 600'; hence, many stadia would be far from the shore and in deep water. Confirmation is given in two of the other gospels. The Gospel of Mark notes that the apostles were "in the middle of the lake" (Mark 6:47), and the Gospel of John notes that the apostles "set off across the lake for Capernaum" and that they had "rowed three and half miles" (John 6:16–19). Realize that the Sea of Galilee is no small lake, being 13 miles long and 8 miles wide, and varying in depth from 165' to 230'.

On top of that, when Peter got out of the boat to walk to Jesus, he sank, crying out, "Lord, save me!" (Matthew 14:30) Again, the water must have been deep for Peter to fear drowning.

Therefore, Jesus was walking on the lake in deep water. Who could do that? None of the apostles ever had such an experience. Nor has anyone else in history!

Raising Lazarus from the dead. This not only points to the divinity of Jesus, but also to the meaning of miracles.

Lazarus lived in Bethany (a village two miles southeast of Jerusalem) with his sisters, Martha and Mary. Jesus was a friend of the family. They believed in Jesus, and so when Lazarus became very ill, "the sisters sent word to Jesus, 'Lord, the one you love is sick'" (John 11:3).

However, Jesus deliberately waited; "Yet when he heard that Lazarus was sick, he stayed where he was for two more days" (John 11:6). Why would he have waited? It seems that he was purposefully waiting until Lazarus died to then perform the greatest of his miracles.

When Jesus finally went to Bethany, Lazarus had been "in the tomb for four days." Martha went to the outskirts of the town to meet Jesus, and with some frustration (maybe even a little anger) she said to him, "Lord, if you had been here, my brother would not have died" (John 11:21). Think about Martha for a moment. Her friend, Jesus, who had performed many miracles, had seemingly taken his time to come. If we guessed what she might have been thinking, it might be something like, "What took you so long? We sent you word. We looked out the window expecting you to show up at any minute, but no, you took your own sweet time."

Still, Martha knew of Jesus's power and so measured her words, saying, "But I know that even now God will give you whatever you ask" (John 11:22).

Jesus tried to make her feel better by telling her that her brother would rise again, and Martha, knowing her scripture (such as Job 19:25–27), said, "I know that he will rise again in the resurrection at the last day" (John 11:24). While she had faith, perhaps it was wavering a bit at the death of her brother, and so Jesus now uttered his famous words, "I am the resurrection and the life. He who believes in me will live, even though he dies; and whoever lives and believes in me will never die. Do you believe this" (John 11:25–26)?

Martha immediately replied, "Yes, Lord, I believe that you are the Christ, the Son of God, who was to come into the world" (John 11:27).

Jesus and Martha then proceeded into Bethany, where Mary repeated Martha's words wishing Jesus had arrived earlier. While not giving her an immediate answer, Jesus saw Mary crying along with many of the friends who had come to comfort Martha and Mary, and he began to also cry. If Jesus waiting for Lazarus to die sounds callous, this moment reveals his true and very loving nature, a man openly weeping over the mourning of his friend. Even the crowd reacted with, "See how he loved him!" (John 11:36)

Then, Jesus moved to the tomb and asked that the stone be taken away that laid across the entrance, causing Martha who was the practical one to comment, "But Lord, by this time there is a bad odor, for he has been there four days" (John 11:39).

But Jesus, knowing the purpose of the miracle then added, "Did I not tell you that if you believed, you would see the glory of God?" (John 11:40), and, "Father, I thank you that you have heard me. I knew that you always hear me, but I said this for the benefit of the people standing here, that they may believe that you sent me" (John 11:41–42). This passage clearly reveals that Jesus is sent by God, the Father, and that he has to prove that by this miracle.

Then, Jesus in a loud voice said, "Lazarus, come out!" Miraculously, Lazarus emerged from the tomb wrapped in his burial cloths. The reaction was strong, "Therefore, many of the Jews who had come to visit Mary, and had seen what Jesus did, put their faith in him" (John 11:43–45).

If you have doubts as to the divinity of Jesus, certainly this miracle must dispel them. And when you combine the fact that Jesus fulfills the prophecies, his identity then being confirmed by the miracles, it must move you to believe all the more. Gradually, his disciples were able to put two and two together, the first to see the truth being Peter (Mark 8:29). Why cannot you also realize who Jesus is?

The resurrection. If you still have doubts, please face the resurrection of Jesus. It is the principal point on which Christianity stands. If Jesus did not rise from the dead, if there was no Easter, then Sundays would be spent in bed instead of in church.

The manner of death will be covered when I answer the question, "Does God Really Love You?" But suffice it to say that it was horrific, crucifixion was so ghastly that it was finally abolished by Emperor Constantine (AD 306–337). The reason Jesus dies in only three hours instead of three days is due to the torture of the scourging at the pillar. While the normal whipping would be limited to thirty-nine lashes (the fear being that more would result in death), the Shroud of Turin reveals more than double that amount. This is why Jesus would drop his cross three times on the way to Golgotha, Simon of Cyrene being forced to carry it for Jesus because the soldiers feared he would die before even reaching the place of crucifixion.

I give you these details as some had claimed that Jesus did not die on the cross, but faked his death, the reason being that normally crucifixion takes many days. However, not only was the death of Jesus hastened by his scourging, but, to make sure he was dead, a soldier thrust a spear into his heart, Saint John even noting, "The man (St. John) who saw it has given testimony, and his testimony is true" (John 19:34–35).

How discouraged and dejected must his apostles have been? A question perhaps in their minds would have been the same one that the chief priests, the teachers of the law, and the elders yelled at him, "'He saved others', they said, 'but he can't save himself! He's the King of Israel! Let him come down now from the cross, and we will believe in him'" (Matthew 27:42; also, Mark 15:31–32; Luke 23:35).

But Jesus does not come down from the cross and dies. He is laid in a tomb, where guards are posted to be sure that his body is not stolen. Three days later, the tomb is empty; Jesus has risen from the dead! (Matthew 28:1–7; Mark 16:1–8; Luke 24:1–12; John 20:1–9)

The gospels then give confirmation of his resurrection, it being noted that Jesus appears to

- Mary Magdalene (Mark 16:9–11; John 20:10–18), to two

- disciples on the road to Emmaus (Mark 16:12–13; Luke 24:13–35), to the
- apostles behind locked doors (Luke 24:36–43; John 20:19–23), to the
- apostles including Thomas (Mark 14:14; John 20:24–31), and to the
- apostles while fishing (John 21:1–14).

It is also reported that Jesus

- asks Peter to feed his sheep (John 21:15–25),
- gives the apostles the Great Commission to preach to all nations (Matthew 28:16–20; Mark 16:15–18), and then
- ascends into heaven in front of them (Mark 16:19–20; Luke 24:50–53).

Still Skeptical?

Are you still not convinced? Do you think that the apostles were lying so as to gain fame and notoriety?

Well, then why would they go to their deaths maintaining it was true? To be a believer in Christ, to believe that he was a king and the Son of God, was blasphemy to the Jews, but treason to the Romans. Belief in Jesus was a capital offense, causing the believer to be executed. Would they die for a lie? Would you?

And they suffered not just any deaths. Consider how they died.

- Peter was crucified upside down in Rome in AD 64.
- Andrew, the brother of Peter, was crucified in Patras, Greece, on a saltire cross (form of an X), year uncertain.
- James the Greater, the brother of John, was beheaded by Herod Agrippa in AD 42. He was the first of the apostles to be martyred.
- James the Less, the first bishop of Jerusalem, was taken around the year AD 62 to the pinnacle of the temple, asked to recant his belief before the assembled crowd, and, when

he refused, was thrown to his death. When discovering the fall had not killed him, he was then beaten to death with clubs.

- Bartholomew was flayed alive and then beheaded. If you ever go to the Sistine Chapel and see Michelangelo's painting of the Last Judgment, there is Bartholomew below Jesus, holding his own skin!
- Matthew was said to have been martyred in Ethiopia or Persia.
- Paul, the Apostle to the Gentiles, was beheaded in Rome in AD 67.

Now, if you were going to be put to death for maintaining that Jesus did rise from the dead, and you knew it was not true, would you not recant to save your life? Of course you would. But they did not. Does that not help you believe? What more do you want?

A Final Point

Add to the above,

- Two thousand years of theology, with such greats as Augustine, Aquinas, and Abelard, and that is just the *As*.
- Also add the great churches that were constructed

   o   St. Peter's in Rome
   o   St. Mark's in Venice
   o   St. Paul's in London
   o   Notre Dame in Paris
   o   St. Basil's in Moscow
   o   St. Stephen's in Vienna
   o   Washington Cathedral in Washington
   o   St. Patrick's and St. John's Cathedrals in New York
   o   And many, many more.

- The faith of your own family, your parents, grandparents, great-grandparents, etc.

Put it all together, and it should do more than put a dent in your doubt; it should move you to faith!

3

Does God Really Love You?

Introduction

Does God really love you? In a "dog eat dog" society built on competition and materialism, where you learn to beat the other before the other beats you, you have become cynical and you feel alone. You have the skepticism of a Doubting Thomas, who needs to see it to believe it.

Well, Holy Week is for you. This is a time when we reflect on the saying that "No greater love has a man than to lay down his life for another." But our reflection is different, unique. While the Passover helps the Jews to remember how in the past the wrath of God passed over the Israelites and struck the first born of Egypt, we do more than just remember. For Christians, the Eucharist has as its purpose to not simply remember how Jesus sacrificed his life for our salvation, but rather to relive it. Theologians use the word *Anamnesis*, which roughly translated means, "making effective in the present an event of the past." When we celebrate the Eucharist, it is as if we are back in AD 33; it is as if we are standing at the foot of the cross and learning what love really means.

When I was a boy, I can remember looking through my uncle's Bible on his coffee table and finding a picture of Jesus being nailed to the cross. His back was arched in pain, and he was screaming. It suddenly dawned on me that while Jesus was God, he was also fully human, and that to have gone through the agony of the cross out of love for you and me made my heart well up with love for him. After ordination, I spent a number of years trying to understand the events of the passion well enough to speak to the hearts of parishioners as that picture once spoke to me.

Let us now recall just how much Jesus really loves you:

1. A Need for Friends

    Jesus had predicted his own suffering. At the Last Supper, he looked Judas in the eye, knowing that he was his betrayer. Now, in the Garden of Gethsemane, he hopes to ready himself through prayer with his friends, the apostles. However, they, exhausted from walking that day from Bethany [where Jesus had left his mother in the care of Martha and Mary] to Jerusalem, have all fallen asleep, and even though he awakens them with a plea, their spirits being willing cannot overcome the weakness of their flesh, and they lapse back into sleep, leaving Jesus all alone.

2. Sweating Blood (Haematidrosis)

    He is so scared that veins just beneath his skin (the subcutaneous capillaries) dilate so broadly that, when they come into contact with the sweat glands, they burst. Jesus literally sweats blood.

3. Death Coming from a Distance

    He then looks out at the scene of Judas coming with Sadducees (the priestly protectors of the law) and Pharisees (the separatists who protect both oral and written tradition), and with both Jewish temple guards and Roman soldiers, the latter sent by Pilate to appease a very demanding and manipulative Caiaphas, the high priest. The soldiers at the beginning and end of the procession carry torches, it thus being very easy to see them coming from a distance, moving ever closer to the inevitable confrontation. Seeing them coming from a distance, he and his apostles could have escaped, but Jesus knew and was committed to his redemptive and loving service.

4. Betrayed at Night

They come at night, because they fear taking Jesus by day will cause a riot among his many supporters, who have seen the miracles and who hope he is the new Messiah.

5. Betrayed by a Kiss

- After three years of observing these miracles and having the luxury of daily listening to Jesus, how does Judas betray Jesus? With a kiss! Jesus looks straight into his eyes, and says, "Judas, with a kiss you betray the Son of Man?"
- As the soldiers move forward to arrest Jesus, broad-shouldered, impetuous Peter lunges forward with a sword, aims at the neck of the servant of the high priest, Malchus, who, seeing Peter coming, turns his head, the result being his ear being sheared off. Jesus tells Peter to sheath his sword, puts his hand over Malchus' head, who is then instantly healed.
- Nonetheless, Jesus is still arrested, all the soldiers drawing their swords, and the disciples quickly scattering, Jesus then has his hands tied behind his back, and a rope placed around his neck, which is tugged to make him hurry. If he slackens his pace or falls, he is kicked.

6. Walking All Night

Imagine how tired Jesus must have been, having been up all day, having walked from Bethany to Jerusalem, and whose Last Supper was Thursday evening. Think of his itinerary:

a. *Annas*

- The Temple is closed, and so Jesus is first brought to the house of the father-in-law of Caiaphas, Annas, as he is the power behind the

High Priest, Caiaphas being the last of six high priests to be appointed by Annas, the other five being Annas's sons. Caiaphas would be the high priest from AD 18–36.

- Allowing this to occur is a sign of respect by Caiaphas to Annas, and is not that inconvenient, as time must occur for all the Sanhedrin to be assembled at Caiaphas' house, which is next-door, a great courtyard being in front of these homes, this being where Peter, who has followed from a distance, now gets questioned himself as to whether he is, or is not, a disciple of the prisoner. It is after Peter has denied Christ a third time that Jesus is now moved from Annas' home to Caiaphas', Jesus simply looking sorrowfully into Peter's eyes illumined by the light of the courtyard fire, who, knowing what he has done, runs away consumed with tears.

b. *Caiaphas*

- The law maintained that not less than twenty-three members of the Great Sanhedrin could try a capital case. They were generally in two groups, those called high priests who actually served the high priest in looking over religious matters, and the elders, men from distinguished families.
- Two members do not attend, Joseph of Arimathea and Nicodemus, because they are friends of the accused.
- A few people are brought in to testify against Jesus, but their testimony is contradictory.
- Jesus is then asked why he teaches heresy and who and how many are his disciples. Jesus remains silent, and hoping to loosen his tongue, a guard slaps his face.

- When finally Caiaphas asks Jesus if he is the Christ, the Son of the Blessed One, Jesus answers, "I am," Caiaphas rends his garments and screams, "What further proof do we need. He has blasphemed!"
- Judges came by him one by one, some spitting in his face, others clenching their fists in rage and hitting him. He said nothing, but the force of these blows may well have caused him to double over in pain. Some laugh at Jesus, who is now bruised and dirty, his eyes puffy from blows, not at all looking like someone who dares call himself the king of the Jews.

c. *Jail Cell*

- He must then have been placed in a jail cell to await going before Pilate in the morning, as the Sanhedrin could sentence someone to death, but only Rome had the ability to carry out the verdict.
- Before being placed in his cell, it is known that the soldiers mocked him, blindfolding him, slapping his face, and then telling him to reveal who did it, if, indeed, he is a Prophet and the Messiah, the Son of God.
- For a time thereafter, he must be alone, waiting for dawn to break, knowing that he will be executed on this final day of his life, and again, filled with fear. He must center himself with prayer, remembering the purpose of life to get through these moments.

d. *Pilate*

- When led before the procurator, Pilate feels caught in a political trap. On one hand, he does not see Jesus as guilty of anything other than being foolish, certainly not a crime punishable by death. On the other hand, two years beforehand, Caiaphas and Annas had both reported Pilate to Tiberius through the Legate of Syria, revealing that Pilate had placed the shields of soldiers bearing the image of Caesar on the outer walls of the Fortress Antonia, in contradiction of an earlier judgment by Tiberius to not carry these votive shields as they unnecessarily offended the Jews and risked rebellion.

- Having been embarrassed by Caiaphas and Annas, Pilate decides to return the embarrassment and hopefully delay the death of Jesus until after midnight, as this was the Day of Preparation, the day before the Sabbath, knowing that Jesus could not be executed on the Sabbath, this effectively delaying the execution until the eight-day Passover concluded.
- Also, he feared risking another blunder, and so decided to throw the ball to Herod Antipas, Tetrarch of Galilee, referring the case to him.

e.   *Herod Antipas*

- He was staying at the Hasmonean Palace, having arrived from Galilee three days earlier to sacrifice at the Temple for the Passover.
- While this was only about two thousand feet away, again Jesus is pulled and kicked, arriving even more exhausted than before, breathing with his mouth wide open as to try to take in more air to survive the moment.
- Herod, aptly named "The Fox," was a man of medium height with a large belly and a square beard. He always wore the trappings of his office: crown, royal cape, and scepter.

- He hoped to see a miracle by this man of whom he had so often heard, this miracle then convincing Herod who he really was. When Jesus not only refused to perform a miracle, but also to even speak, Herod became incensed. He insulted him, walking around Jesus, making personal remarks about his shabby clothing, his lacerated face, his dirty garments, and the now unwashed face and swollen eyes.
- To even more insult Jesus, he had a royal cape put around Jesus, mocking him with the contrast of a royal garment on top such a mess of a man. Everyone began to laugh.
- Then Herod ordered Jesus back to Pilate, The Fox not falling for the trap set by Pilate. Jesus, with exhaustion, turns to head back, now having stood for many hours.

f. *Pilate a Second Time.* Now Pilate decides to try one last maneuver, to have Jesus scourged with the hope that the crowd will be moved to pity.

7. Scourging at the Pillar

- Jesus was stripped to the waist; he was forced to kneel in front of a small three-foot post, to which his hands are tied. A bag was placed over his head so as to increase his fear at not knowing when the blow would come, or from which direction.
- The whip (the "flagellum") was a cat-of-nine tails; this had two leather thongs extending from the wooden base, with a jagged stone (or bits of bone) near the end so as to bruise the skin, and with the thong then dividing into nine parts so as to cut the skin.
- The most severe beating was to be thirty-nine lashes, as it was believed that forty lashes might kill a person.

The Shroud of Turin reveals that Jesus had received more than twice the normal beating. Jewish floggings were kept to thirty-nine lashes (thirteen on each shoulder + thirteen on the loins). Roman floggings had no such limitations. The scourging would only take three minutes.

- It is believed that the beating was so severe that fluid formed around the heart of Jesus, creating intense pain, and giving the logic for why he would fall with the cross three times along the way of the cross, as he would feel like he was having a heart attack.

- It also explains why he died in three hours instead of three days, as was often the case. And it was this pericardial fluid that came out of his side when it was lanced by the centurion, not blood and water, but blood and pericardial fluid.

8. Crown of Thorns

The soldiers then sat Jesus up, as he was trying to catch his breath, and made fun of he who would be called King of the Jews. They put an old and dirty scarlet, wool cloak ("sagum") over his now open wounds, blindfolded him again, and, again made him guess who was slapping him or spitting at him. They put a heavy reed in his hand as his scepter. And then, they took those long thorns that were often used as kindling for a fire, and fashioned a crown, pressing this crown into the flesh of his head. His face would soon be covered with blood, it therefore being no miracle that when Veronica wipes the face of Jesus that his image appears on the cloth. His face was literally soaked with blood!

9. The Unwavering Crowd

- When Jesus is led back to Pilate, even he and the crowd are shocked. As the mood of the crowd has not changed, Pilate tries one last maneuver to attempt saving Jesus, showing him to the crowd and yelling, "Ecce Homo!," which means, "Behold the man!"

- But the crowd is unwavering, and even when offered the choice of Jesus, who cured their sick, or Barabbas, a common criminal, to be freed as was the custom at Passover, they choose Barabbas, shouting to Pilate that if he does not allow Jesus to be crucified, having before him a man who claimed to be a King rivaling Caesar, it is treason, knowing full well that Caiaphas will spin the story that way to once again embarrass him.

- Accordingly, being out of options, Pilate condemns Jesus to death, and symbolically washes his hands of the sentence, the crowd gleefully yelling, "Let it be upon our heads and the heads of our children."

- He then ordered that over the head of Jesus on the cross be placed, as was the custom, both his name and his crime, hence, "Jesus of Nazareth, King of the Jews," written in Hebrew, Latin, and Aramaic, in that order. We simply see depictions of the initials, "INRI."

10. The Way of the Cross

- Jesus then has to walk about three thousand feet up a steep hill (via doloroso) through the Gennath Gate and then, once through the gate, about thirty yards to Golgotha, carrying the thirty-pound crossbeam (patibulum) over his shoulders. It was three by five inches wide and six feet long.

- The upright beam (stipes curcis) was left permanently at the place of execution, the crossbeam being attached when the criminal arrived. It was six feet tall.

- So Jesus picks up a heavy weight—after no sleep, a long walk, being on his feet for hours, and having endured a savage beating—and proceeds to *Calvary* (the Latin term for *skull*; Golgotha being Aramaic), the crowd easily being able to hear his labored breathing.

- The road is not smooth, and in his exhaustion, Jesus falls three times, scraping his knees, elbows, and hands as he does. Four soldiers are assigned to each criminal, but the centurion, Abenadar, fearing that Jesus will die before arriving at Golgotha, forces an onlooker who was a visiting farmer, Simon of Cyrene, to carry the cross the rest of the way.

11. Golgotha

They finally arrive at Golgotha, which is Aramaic for "Place of the Skull" (the Latin term being *calvariae locus* from which the English term *Calvary* comes, this being from the Greek *kraniou topos*). It is called that as bodies are frequently left to rot, not being claimed by family, and skulls and bones litter the area. It is just outside a city gate, bodies often being left on the cross, even after death, to have those entering the city each day know that if they break the law, this could happen to them.

12. Stripped Naked

Jesus is then stripped of all his clothes, part of the punishment being the indignity of hanging naked before others, and knowing that rats, dogs, and birds would pick at your remains, including your genitals. The soldiers will cast lots for his robe, this often being the custom, and serving as a tip for a job well done.

13. Nailed to the Cross

- Crucifixion is a manner of death for slaves or non-Romans for such crimes as murder, piracy, treason, or rebellion. So brutal was this form of death that Constantine eventually abolished it.

- Jesus is laid on the ground while his wrists vs. his hands are nailed to the crossbeam, as the bone structure of the hands would not support a person's weight, causing them to fall off the cross. Of the four soldiers for each prisoner, two soldiers hold down each arm (kneeling on the inner elbow and holding down his arm with their two hands) while another pounds the nails into place. The nails were five inches long. The soldiers then elevate and attach the crossbeam to the upright beam, finally nailing his feet with his knees in a bent position.

- On the cross would be either a peg to rest his feet, or one to rest his body, or both. This would be for the purpose of extending the death, as the criminal would have to push himself up over rough-hewn wood to be able to breathe, the muscles of his arms and legs in spasm as he tries to survive a moment longer.

- The assembled crowd would be mesmerized with alternating horror and glee to see the side show of a man struggling to raise himself so as to breathe. If he passed out, he would slump, be unable to breathe, and quickly awaken. Eventually, being so weak, he would slump and suffocate.

- Imagine the feelings experienced by Mary as she watches her son, whom she had bathed as a baby and for whom she had cared as a boy, who himself had healed others, ending their pain, now being tortured to death.

14. Manner of Death

Death is not caused from loss of blood, but rather from asphyxiation. For, when your arms are over your head, your diaphragm crowds your lungs, and it becomes increasingly difficult to breathe. To slow the death, pegs to rest the feet and body would be provided. To hurry the death, the legs of the criminal would be broken, forcing the criminal to slump, suffocate, and die. Jesus's feet are only one to two feet off the ground, low enough for a soldier to offer wine mixed with gall, which was a narcotic to dull the pain. Jesus refused it.

15. "It is Finished!"

Three hours later, the beating hurries his death, and he cries out in a loud voice, "It is finished!" This is a cry of victory, not of despair. He has triumphed in his struggle to live a life without sin so as to redeem you and me. He has never abandoned his love for his father, and has always shown kindness to all whom he has met, even those who crucified him, with the astounding statement, "Father forgive them for they know not what they do." He has, indeed, to paraphrase St. Paul, fought the good fight, run the race, and resisted temptation.

Conclusion

But it is not finished for you and me. And so, when we are tempted to fall, to choose evil over good, we must call to mind the example and love of Christ. Then, we must return to our daily lives with a renewed sense of purpose and hope. In a world that doubts whether anyone really cares, you must be a living sacrament, a living sign of God's love for us by the way you love others.

In the Eucharist, the celebrant proclaims, "Christ our Passover is sacrificed for us," to which we answer, "Therefore, let us keep the feast." The question today is: Do you keep the feast? Do you act like a sacrament, a sign of love to your neighbor? Are you a Christian? Are you like Christ?

Be moved by love; be moved to improve your love of others so that just as the people of Antioch first called the disciples of Christ "Christians," noting "See how they love one another," people today will be able to throw away their doubt and cynicism in the face of your love. Let each day of your life demonstrate a life of love to all whom you meet: your parents, your teacher, your spouse, your children, your employer, and even the person sitting next to you in church.

4
What Is the Purpose of Your Life?

We all wonder what the purpose of our life is. The issue is so big that it scares us, causing us to avoid facing it, the result being that one day this repressed issue comes frighteningly bubbling to the surface. As the answer is essential to determine how we shall pursue happiness, let us look at it honestly instead of ducking it. So why were you born?

To Live Forever? No. You can eat healthy foods until they come out of your ears, exercise to the point of making Arnold Schwarzenegger jealous, drink the standard eight glasses of water a day, have more cosmetic surgery than Cher and Demi Moore combined, and one hundred years from now, you will be dead.

To Become Rich? No. Oh, don't get me wrong. Material wealth is nice to have, but you must share it, and you cannot take it with you. I have often joked with people that their Lexus will not fit into their coffin with them, but their soul will, it being ironic how much time we spend on things that do not last. Think of all the riches that were buried with the Pharaohs to help them on the journey to the next life, only to have people in this life steal them.

To Become Famous? No. Read *People* magazine. Fame is fleeting. The adoration of the masses can leave as quickly as it comes, and can be falsely placed, based on performance instead of personality, and occasionally based on behavior that is more ignominious than renown.

To Have Power? No. Again, that does not endure. Think of Alexander the Great, Caesar, and Napoleon. They conquered, or tried to conquer, the world. But today, they are but a memory. Reflect upon Percy Bysshe Shelley's 1817 poem, "Ozymandias," where he contemplates on a decaying statue of Ramses II, contrasting the arrogant words of the ancient Pharaoh *("My name is Ozymandias, king of kings. Look on my works, ye Mighty and despair!")* with the sorry state and empty surroundings of his statue *("Nothing else remains, Round the decay of that colossal wreck").*

To Love and Be Loved? Yes. You are defined by the choices you make. Each interaction with each person on each day of your life is an opportunity for you to grow or shrink, to love or hate. You can be kind or cruel, helpful or manipulative, cooperative or controlling.

Happiness

What then is happiness? It is a process, not a product. It is not something you buy, but a process of becoming. You do not have to be a corporate executive, make a six-figure income, and drive a BMW to be happy. These things are certainly nice, but my point is that what you attain is less important than how you attain it. It is how we relate to others that determines our degree of happiness.

Think about it. You are loved by your spouse and children not for all the hours you worked or goodies you provided, but rather for those qualities that made spending time with you a joy, such as your sensitivity, caring, reliability, and responsibility. Those qualities are internal. They are part of you, defining who you are, your very soul. Both this life and the next will be enriched or impoverished by the depth of those qualities, rewarding you with the closeness of friends or punishing you with the loneliness of a selfish heart. The judgment of God will be to simply accept your own free will judgment, made over a lifetime to be experienced for eternity.

Therefore, you were born to become fully human, fully mature, and fully happy. Who you are inside will go with you from this life to the next. What you have on the outside, whether possessions or acclaim, will not. Do not despair for not having enough of the latter, but for your sake, seize every day you have left to add to the former, to add to who you are meant to become, a work of art.

A Picture of Heaven and Hell

Still a bit confused? Well, let us look at this from another angle. My belief is that the purpose of life is to make a simple choice between good or evil, our answer being shown less by what we say and more by what we do, our actions speaking louder than our words. For those who are religious, those choices on earth affect how we shall live after death.

If you choose to view others as suckers of whom you can take advantage instead of as potential friends, then you fail to learn how to be close to them, condemning yourself to be lonely, frustrated, and angry. When you are placed in the presence of God after death, never having learned how to be close to others, you do not know how to be close to God, nor to all who have died before you: your mom and dad, brothers and sisters, uncles and aunts, and all your friends. Then you look around and see many who are close, and, therefore, happy. All of a sudden, you realize that this state of emptiness will last for all eternity. You are in hell.

However, if during your lifetime, you give of yourself and thus receive love and friendship in return, you may not be rich or famous, but you will possess the secret of life, that is, knowing how to love. When placed in the presence of God and of all your family and friends, you will be able to be close to them, your reward being eternal happiness. You are in heaven.

Still too complicated? Then on the premise that a picture is worth a thousand words, here is the answer that I gave to a little boy who once asked me what heaven and hell were like. It worked so well that now I use it with adults.

I told him to imagine entering into a big house in which there were only two rooms, one marked "Heaven" and one marked "Hell."

First, you look into the room marked "Hell." You see a large banquet table with all your favorite foods: turkey with all the fixings, roast beef, ham, corn, peas, ice cream, cakes, pies, and everything your heart desires. There are no liver, lima beans, or brussels sprouts. But all the knives, forks and spoons are eight feet long, and you cannot eat without using the utensils. So hell is being so close and yet so far from all that luscious food.

Then you peek into the room marked "Heaven." It is the same picture! All your favorite foods are set before you, and you must use the eight-foot utensils to eat. But because you were caring instead of selfish during your lifetime, it occurs to you that you can reach out and feed the person sitting across from you.

Hence, those in heaven are having a party, where those in hell are starving to death, worrying how they are going to get that food into their mouths without the other people stealing it from them.

The situation is the same, but the two groups see it differently, having learned to love or not love during their lives on earth. One can easily see the solution; the other is blind.

Conclusion

God gives us free will. The judgment of God is to accept your judgment. The punishment for choosing to be selfish is to be selfish. It saddens God if you choose to not love Him or your fellow human beings, but that is your choice. You choose to be happy or sad, to be in heaven or hell. He provides eternal life. You determine how you will live it.

You should not wait to make this choice on your deathbed, but do so every day of your life. If you are on the wrong path, then wake up and change! If you are on the right path, then do not become smug and complacent, just keep going. Go to church or synagogue to continue to learn more about the purpose of life and be refreshed for the challenges of each day. Then love your family, give an honest day's labor at work, treat all people as you would want to be treated, and worry not about the end of this life. The next one will be very happy.

Note: The answer to this question was taken from my first book, *Map to Happiness: Straightforward Advice on Everyday Issues* (New York: iUniverse, 2008, 2–5).

5
Why Does God Allow Suffering?

If our growth during life is to choose who we shall be as determined by how we relate to others, does not suffering get in the way, muddying the waters?

No, actually, quite the opposite, suffering is part of the process. Suffering is inevitable. The question is not whether we shall suffer, but how shall we respond when suffering eventually comes our way.

If you think that you are being punished for something you did wrong in your life, that just is not true. Consider some examples given us from the Bible of the suffering of many wonderful people.

1. *Abraham* made the arduous journey from Mesopotamia to Canaan, then suffered ridicule from his own wife that he would be the father of a multitude, and finally thought that God wanted him to sacrifice his son, Isaac.
2. *Abel* was murdered by his brother, Cain, for being favored by God for offering a lamb instead of spoiled grain and fruit to God.
3. *Noah* suffered the ridicule of his townspeople for building an ark in an arid country during a particularly long dry season.
4. *Jeremiah* boldly spoke out for years (627–587 BC) against the kings of Judah (Jehoiakim, Jehoichin, and Zedekiah) for the worship of false gods, opposing other prophets who said that their dreams revealed that Judah could conquer

any nation, even the empire of Babylon. What was his reward—suffering.

a. People spat on him, laughed at him.
b. He was put in a stockade for all to ridicule him. He became so depressed that he wished that his mother had aborted him!
c. He was imprisoned, once in a cistern that was filthy.
d. He was flogged.
e. He decided to never marry, so a wife and children would not have to suffer.
f. He was stoned to death in Egypt.

5. *Job*—a story about a man who lives a sinless life, and yet loses his farm, his animals, his children, and his health, his wife cynically telling him to just "curse God and die"; but, he remains faithful, even when he cannot fully understand what is happening to him. This story spoke to the very souls of the people of his time, a people who did not have the insights that we do from the life, death and resurrection of Jesus Christ.

6. *Jesus*

a. Born in a manger instead of a palace, wrapped in swaddling clothes instead of silk,
b. Grew up in the town of Nazareth, which was so small and obscure it was not even mentioned in the Old Testament,
c. Worked the hard life of a carpenter, and then, after years of miracles for others, was
d. Flogged at the pillar, receiving more than twice the normal number of lashes, before suffering the barbarity and ignominy of being crucified.

7. *Peter*—crucified upside down.

8. *Paul*

    a.   Imprisoned, flogged, evicted from many towns, shipwrecked, and beheaded.

    b.   And on top of this, he suffered continually with what he described as his "thorn of the flesh," thought to be either malaria or epilepsy.

    c.   All this happening to a man whom history tells us was short, fat, bald, and sickly, not the tall, dark, and handsome man depicted in many paintings and statues.

9. *James, the brother of John*—beheaded with an axe.
10. *James the Less*—thrown off the pinnacle of the Temple for not renouncing Christ, and then beaten to death with clubs at the base of temple, as he was still alive.
11. *Bartholomew*—flayed alive. Michelangelo's "The Last Judgment" over the high altar in the Sistine Chapel depicts Bartholomew just below Jesus holding his own skin!

So many good people so wrongly treated, and not because they did something bad.

Certainly, my own life has been anything but free from suffering. Not only was my life scarred by the death of my father when I was fourteen, but my first wife, Nicki, was sick for twenty-one years before dying of an auto-immune disease that could not even be stemmed by a liver transplant.

And in 1972, five weeks after my ordination, I was involved in a car accident where my car rolled over six times, leaving me for the rest of my life with a bad back that forced me to exercise for an hour each morning so as to be able to function. The woman who caused the accident fled the scene. She sped away, leaving me in a field to die, and, while I was lucky to live, it always irked me to know that she "got away with it," although I know that her own behavior must have haunted her.

But the central question to which everyone returns over and over again is why must we all get sick and die, whether it be from cancer, a heart attack, a stroke, or arthritis that causes us to have knee-and-hip replacements or any other ailment?

What reasons can there be for such suffering? Why would God do that to us? What is the theology of suffering? Here are some reasons that I have discovered, and have helped me cope.

1. *To wake us up.* We are so consumed with our daily lives that we often forget that life does not last. Suffering is an inescapable wake-up call reminding us of our mortality.

2. *To help us grow*

   a. Once awakened, suffering confronts our often confused and self-centered values and priorities, and makes us realize that material goods, no matter how wonderful, do not last. Suffering makes us re-evaluate our lives, paying more attention to our inner growth that travels with us from this life to the next, instead of our outer possessions that remain here after we die. In sermons, I have often quipped, "your Lexus will not fit into the coffin with you, but your soul will. On which one are you spending more time?"

   b. Another way, less popular, to describe this reasoning would be that it is "to discipline us." Discipline is defined by Webster's dictionary as "training expected to produce a specific type or pattern of behavior." God loves us and wants what is best for us. After all, to the degree to which we grow on earth is the degree to which we shall live for eternity. The judgment of God is simply to accept our judgment in terms of how we chose to live during our lives, based upon a lifetime of daily choices. God does not whimsically punish us. God simply enforces the consequences of our own choices, eternally. As this is very serious, and as we can easily travel down the wrong road in life, to be disciplined by God is not such a bad thing. When our parents disciplined us, we rethought our behavior. Suffering does the same.

3. *To achieve higher levels of growth*

    a. Suffering proves our character, integrity, and the depth of our faith (James 1:2). After all, life is hard. Paul referred to life as a struggle, saying upon death that we have run the race and fought the fight (2 Timothy 4:7).
    b. Suffering occurs throughout our lives, intensifying as we reach the end of our lives. But, during our lifetime, suffering makes us realize that the degree of our difficulty in dealing with suffering is related to the level of our growth. The more we grow, we not only become happier, but also more mature, and thus better able to withstand the inevitable vicissitudes of life.
    c. It is not enough to dust off a pew once a week. A deeper faith, one that will be needed when bad times come our way, needs a lifetime of work. To make this point, Jesus tells the parable of the farmer who scatters seed that falls on four different types of ground: the path, rocky soil, thorny soil, and good soil. Its interpretation speaks to all humanity (Matthew 13:3–23).

        i.   Those who blindly make no effort to even explore the claims of a spiritual life are left with a religious void. A person can grow up with parents who never attend church, but he or she is still aware that others do. If he then makes no effort to even look into that sphere of life, he condemns himself to an inner emptiness, a life with no depth (the path).
        ii. Those who are armed with only whatever they were taught in Sunday school have very little depth, and their shallow faith, when challenged by our cynical world that unrealistically demands

        material proofs of something spiritual, can instill doubt (rocky soil).

iii. Those who may go to church, but rarely dust off the Bible sitting on their coffee table lose their faith when the thorns of a serious illness enter their lives (thorny soil).

iv. Those who explore the meaning of life and work to resolve their doubts are able to grow, even amidst the trials and tribulations of life (good soil).

This means that you have to work at your relationship with God. Think of the example of marriage. Does a bad argument mean that you divorce your spouse? Do you not try to work through your troubles, and in doing so, strengthen your marriage? Well, it is the same with God. Will illness force you to divorce God? Why not work through the challenges of life to deepen your faith and your happiness.

4. *To develop hope*

a. "Suffering produces perseverance, perseverance produces character, and character produces hope" (Romans 5:3–4).

b. The more that suffering enters your life, the more aware you become of the fact that "this cannot be all that there is." Would God give us all a desire to be perfectly happy and then not make that possible? That would only make God cruel. But, God, by his very definition as being good, would not do that. Hence, the limits of this life in contrast to our desire for full happiness produce a hope for more, for eternal life and eternal happiness. Deductive reasoning in philosophy tells us that it is true, and faith reassures us that what we hope for is real.

5. *To develop feelings of sympathy and empathy for others* (2 Corinthians 1:3–5). If you have ever been in the hospital, ever experienced a bad back or arthritis, ever been through chemotherapy, ever had a heart attack or a stroke, then your empathy and sympathy for others suffering the same is deep and comforting to them and you.

6. *To confront pride*

   a. Paul's "thorn of the flesh" helped him to maintain a spirit of humility (2 Corinthians 12:7).
   b. Pride is becoming too wrapped up in this life instead of seeing more clearly this life in contrast to the next, to seeing the material world that will pass away in contrast to the spiritual world that will endure forever, in seeing the power of muscles and beauty for a brief time in your life contrasted with the eternal power and majesty of an omnipotent God.

7. *To make manifest the evil of others*

   a. If we are persecuted, our suffering makes the evil in others clear for all to see, including God (1 Thessalonians 2:14–16).
   b. If someone cruelly makes fun of you, or derides you in front of others, you are hurt, but the other is hurt even more, for we all see just how mean and cruel that person really is.
   c. If we think of the horrors of war, of the extermination of millions of Jews at the hands of Nazi Germany, we wonder how God could allow such a thing. But God gives us free choice. And as I said above, while God does not interfere with the choices we make, he holds our feet to the fire with the consequences of those choices, eternally!

8. *To provide an opportunity to witness, give testimony* When we enter the process of dying, some people will expect us to despair and toss aside our faith. However, if we show others our steadfast, unwavering faith even in the face of death, then others who witness our suffering may rethink their atheism or agnosticism.

   a. The Romans were shocked to see the Christians singing in the coliseum instead of despairing.

   b. When I was twenty-five and just ordained a deacon, I went to visit a cousin of mine, Peggy, who, at age forty-eight, was dying of cancer.

      As I was with her in the hospital, our uncle, a big, burly state trooper, came in to visit her. He had long since stopped going to church, and no matter how much his mother and father, brothers and sisters, his wife, and his own children begged him to return to church, he stubbornly would not.

      In the hospital room, he saw Peggy saying the rosary, and scoffed, "A lot of good that's doing you." Peggy, unable to speak above a whisper, having been on a ventilator, signaled to him. He lowered his ear to her face, and she simply said, "I believe." Our uncle backed away, saying nothing, and left the room.

      Peggy died two days later, and our uncle then began to go back to church. I was always amazed that Peggy, unable to even speak above a whisper or even lift her arms off the bed, was able to move the mountain that was our uncle, all because her belief was strong in the face of a body that was weak and dying. Her witness produced a change that no other person had been able to do.

Conclusion

While all of this may still sound unfair, remember that our parents disciplined us for our own good (to respect other children, to not cheat at school, to tell the truth, to not eat sweets before dinner so we could eat a healthy meal, etc.) We may have been angry to be disciplined, and even rebelled by slamming doors or telling our parents that we hated them. But, after we grew up, we knew that they did this for our own good. For if we did not learn those lessons when young, our bad behaviors would come back to bite us when older.

And were we not tested over and over again to prove that we were ready to graduate and take a job? We never liked being tested, but no one would hand us a diploma or job if we had not been through that process.

God is our Father, and suffering is his discipline for us.

But realize that the hold of materialism over us is very strong. A shiny car, a big house, a big promotion, an expensive vacation, all are so manifest and screaming in our ear of their importance. Whereas, spiritual growth and the promise of eternal happiness sound like so much pie in the sky.

And while every sermon by every priest in every church on every Sunday has its purpose to remind us of what really matters, our churches are half-full at best on Sundays, and so we material beings need not only a spiritual reminder about the purpose of life, but also a material kick in the pants—suffering.

Therefore, suffering does not mean that God is picking on you. Quite the opposite. It does not mean that you should rejoice in suffering but to read the signs and contemplate the meaning of suffering and, by that, the meaning of life.

6

Why Do Bad Things Happen to Good People?

Certainly, this question is related to the issue of suffering. While a wonderful book has been written on this topic by Rabbi Harold Kushner (*When Bad Things Happen to Good People*, New York, Anchor Books, 1981), a book I would encourage you to read, I shall approach the answer to this question from a somewhat different angle.

I mentioned earlier in this book that the Bible is one process of thinking instead of many interesting, but often confusing, stories. The Bible is written over many centuries during which the understanding of God and life gradually became clearer. Interestingly, the entire Bible moves slowly but inevitably to the answer of this question as to why bad things happen to good people.

The Bible is essentially divided into five sections:

1. **The History Books**
2. **Wisdom Literature**
3. **The Prophets**
4. **The Gospels**
5. **The Epistles**

Let us travel through the Bible to find our answer.

1. **The History Books** (Genesis, Exodus, Joshua, Judges, Samuel, Kings, etc.)

Here, the message is simple, revealing a theory of retribution: if you are bad, you are punished; if you are good, you are rewarded. The rewards will be victory in battle, good health, a long life, a loving wife, and lots of children, land, and animals. The punishment will be to not receive those blessings.

- Adam and Eve eat the apple from the Tree of Knowledge and are booted out of the Garden of Eden.
- Pharaoh does not heed the warnings of Moses, and Egypt is stricken with plagues.
- While Moses is receiving the Ten Commandments atop Mt. Sinai, the Jews are breaking them at the base of Mt. Sinai and are punished by having to wander in the desert for forty years.
- Those who follow God's will are victorious.

    o Joshua conquers Jericho.
    o Gideon defeats the Midianites.
    o Deborah's army defeats King Jabin of Hazor, and
    o David defeats the Philistines.

- Those who do not follow God's will are punished.

    o Samson is blinded, and
    o Saul is killed by the Philistines.

2. **Wisdom Literature** (Wisdom, Ecclesiastes, Ecclesiasticus, Proverbs, Psalms, Job, etc.)

    Here the message is that the theory of retribution does not really work. There are plenty of people who are good, yet suffer, and plenty of people who are bad who prosper and enjoy long lives.

    The central story is Job. While Job is not an actual person, but rather a popular folktale, the story makes clear the problem with the theory of retribution. Job "was blameless and upright; he feared God and shunned evil. He had seven sons and three daughters, and he owned seven thousand sheep, three thousand camels, five hundred yoke of oxen and five hundred donkeys, and had a large number of servants" (Job 1:1–3).

So far, so good. But then, we are observers in the court of God, where Satan comes and goes, being asked by God if he has seen his best creation, Job. Satan maintains that Job is only good because he has a good life. However, if God allows tests to come upon Job, he will despair and curse God. So God allows Satan to visit upon Job all manner of problems: foreigners invade his lands and carry away his animals, a storm collapses the house where his children are and they all die, and finally his health is taken away, being afflicted with "painful sores from the soles of his feet to the top of his head" (Job 2:7). Job's wife even encourages him to "Curse God and die," but he will not. Even with all his troubles, Job remains blameless.

Therefore, the book makes it very clear that the theory of retribution is not working. If Job is good, he should be rewarded, not punished. Well, as the story continues, Job is visited by three friends, who tell him that he must have sinned for such disaster to strike him. However, Job protests that he has not sinned, crying out in frustration that "I am innocent, but God denies me justice. Although I am right, I am considered a liar; although I am guiltless, his arrow inflicts an incurable wound," then concluding "It profits a man nothing when he tries to please God" (Job 34:5–9). Job, like you and me, cries out to God, asking, why are you doing this to me?

God's answer shocks Job. God is angry, beginning by saying, "Who is this obscuring my designs with his empty-headed words? Brace yourself like a fighter; now it is my turn to ask questions and yours to inform me" (Job 38:2–3).

The questions of God are ones only he could answer.

- "Where were you when I laid the earth's foundations" (Job 38:4)?
- "Who pent up the sea behind closed doors" (Job 38:8)?
- "Have you ever in your life given orders to the morning or sent the dawn to its post" (Job 38:12)?
- "Have you ever visited the place where the snow is kept, or seen where the hail is stored up" (Job 38:22)?
- "Do you find a prey for the lioness and satisfy the hunger of her whelps" (Job 38:39)?

Pummeled with questions, Job gets the point, and answers, "I am unworthy—how can I reply to you? I put my hand over my mouth. I spoke once, but I have no answer—twice, but I will say no more" (Job 40:4–5).

God then continues to put Job in his place, confronting Job with his power. "Do you really want to reverse my judgment, and put me in the wrong to put yourself in the right? Has your arm the strength of God's, can your voice thunder as loud" (Job 40:8–9)?

Job in humility finally accepts that God is God and man is man, and Job will have to accept his life as it is. "I know that you can do all things; no plan of yours can be thwarted." "Therefore, I despise myself and repent in dust and ashes" (Job 42:2–6).

Imagine how discouraging that had to be for the people of that era, the essence of the message being, I am God, you are man, and you will have to deal with whatever I choose to do. If there is no reward for doing good, if a blameless man like Job can be punished so severely, then life no longer makes sense.

You might just as well eat, drink and be merry, for tomorrow you may die. (Ecclesiastes 9:7–10)

It is interesting that the Book of Job ends with an insertion that does not seem to fit, namely, where Job gets back double of what he had lost. Some scholars wonder whether this was added at a later time so as to make the theory of retribution work, but the sad point is, it does not work. The basis of morality seems to be shattered.

This same sense of being discouraged, pessimistic, and lost without meaning is reflected in the Book of Ecclesiastes. It describes Solomon, the king who had it all (wives, palaces, soldiers, wisdom, riches), and yet finds life meaningless, "Vanity of vanities. All is vanity! For all his toil, his toil under the sun, what does man gain by it" (Ecclesiastes 1:2–3)? So if the richest and most powerful man that ever lived cannot be happy, what does that say about us?

3. **The Prophets** (Amos, Hosea, Micah, Isaiah, Jeremiah, Ezekiel, Malachi, etc.)

The third section of the Bible tries to make sense of it all. It cannot be that bad. There must be something that we missed. There must be someone coming who can make sense of it all, and set the world right.

So, gradually, as I noted in the answer to the second question, the prophets begin to predict the coming of the Messiah, the Christ, the anointed one, the deliverer.

- Nathan (1000–961 BC) predicts that he will be born in the lineage of King David. *Joseph was a descendant of David.*
- Micah (714–701 BC) predicts that he will be born in Bethlehem, the city where David was born. *Joseph has to return to Bethlehem where he was born to be counted in a census, Jesus then being born there.*
- Isaiah (742–701 BC) predicts that he will be born of a virgin, and that his name will be Emmanuel ("God is with us"). *Mary was a virgin, and Jesus, as we have seen, is the Son of God.*
- Jeremiah (626–587 BC) predicts that he will write his covenant on our hearts instead of on tablets of stone. *Jesus's words do speak to our hearts.*

- Deutero-Isaiah (between 587–540 BC) predicts that he will be a Suffering Servant who will die for our sins. *Jesus dies on the cross.*
- Malachi (between 515–545 BC) predicts that he will be immediately preceded by Elijah who will return to life and shout out in the desert to make straight the way of the Lord. *John the Baptist is dressed in a hair shirt like Elijah and cries out in the desert where he baptizes in preparation of the Messiah.*

4. **The Gospels** (Matthew, Mark, Luke, and John)

Here we finally have Jesus, the Messiah, who can somehow make sense of it all. How frustrated must Jesus have been? He must have shaken his head, when telling us that the theory of retribution does work, but spiritually, not materially! It does not mean that you will live a long life, never suffer, and have lots of kids and possessions. No. Instead, it means that to the extent that you learn to love, to that same extent do you experience happiness.

Is that disappointing to you? It was to the people of Jesus's time. They wanted to have the Messiah be a warrior who would ride into Jerusalem on a steed to proclaim war on Rome. They did not want a carpenter from a poor town ride into Jerusalem on a donkey to proclaim peace.

But that is the problem that we have always had. We are body and soul, but we pay more attention to the body than the soul. We never miss a meal, but we probably rarely pray. We work for a bigger house or car, not so that we can help the poor by tithing to a church or synagogue.

Well, what is in it for you? Why be spiritual? What do you get from being good? What does it mean, "to give is to receive"? Consider the following:

- *Love of others.* Think of your relationship with your spouse and children.

  o What do you get from buying your wife a dozen roses when it is not even her birthday? Her love. She cannot wait for you to get home so she can give you a hug and kiss.

  o What do you get from giving your children a good education, helping them do their homework, consoling them when they get hurt, buying them clothes to wear and a bike to ride? Their love.

  o I once had a man who came into counseling bemoaning the fact that he had only saved a few million dollars by the end of his career, comparing himself with his college roommate who had amassed ten times that amount. I asked about his friend's marriage and children, discovering that he was divorced and rarely saw his adult children. My client had a loving wife and a great relationship with his children and grandchildren. I then asked, who was really rich? He got my point.

- *Inner depth and contentment*

  o Now take a lifetime of offering your love to others, regardless of getting something back. Not only do you have good friends and a loving family, but you also have learned to love so deeply that you experience richness in the quality of those relationships. Love is, after all, a quality, not a quantity. You are known as a person who really cares, and that not only gives respect coming back to you, but an inner contentment. You have felt the power of love, and so you treasure the depth of your soul and the depth of the relationships that allows you to develop.

o And you have learned what really matters. So if you had to choose between a loss on the stock market or the loss of your spouse, it would be an easy choice for you. You would be able to answer Jesus's question, "What does it profit a man to gain the world and lose his soul?" (Mark 8:36) Nothing!

o Think of going to an art museum. One person can look at a work of art, and say, "Okay, next. What's so great about that?" Another person can look at that painting longer and get a deeper sense of joy in what they are experiencing. That is what God wants for you. Don't you want that for yourself?

To the degree that you disagree, or to the degree that you do not even understand what I am saying, it is to that degree that you have to grow.

What does that growth look like? It means realizing what you gain by seeing the true meaning of life. Consider a few examples.

• *Forgiveness*

o We are told to forgive others. Suppose that you do, but they continue to hurt you. Are you a fool? No, you gave that person a chance to grow and still have you in their life. If they choose to not change, they shrink in their ability to connect, not just with you, but also with all people. The punishment for being selfish is to *be* selfish. Whatever pound of flesh you might exact as a punishment is peanuts in comparison to the harm that person does to him or herself.

o However, forgiving does not mean that you have to keep taking the abuse.

- Jesus said, 'Whose sins you shall forgive, they are forgiven them. Whose sins you shall retain, they are retained" (John 20:21–23). We forget the second half of that advice. You do not keep forgiving someone who continues hurting you.

- I made up a story to make my point. Imagine that I punch you in the nose, but then immediately apologize and beg your forgiveness. You know I am a priest, and everyone says I am a nice guy, so you forgive me. Immediately, I punch you in the nose again, causing blood to flow down your face. I now kneel in front of you, begging you to forgive me, claiming that I shall never do it again. Reluctantly, you forgive me a second time only to have me punch you a third time. In response, you raise your fists and tell me to get away from you. Are you being un-Christian? No, you are being un-stupid! You may hope that I shall change, but you are not going to become my punching bag.

- But Jesus said that we should forgive 70 x 7 times? (Matthew 18:22). Remember, however, that Jesus preached in hyperbole, that is, by exaggeration to make a point. He did not mean that you have to forgive someone 490 times, just that you should try to forgive more than you do, realizing that sinners do more harm to themselves than to you.

- *Humility.* Here is another virtue that we misunderstand. Many think that to be humble is to eat humble pie, to never assert themselves, instead always deferring to whatever others wish to do.

No, that would make you weak. By contrast, humility makes you strong, as it is really seeing yourself in contrast to God. God is eternal; you are limited to one time. God is omnipresent; you are limited to one place. God is omnipotent; your power is limited. God is omniscient; your knowledge is limited.

It is that contrast that makes us bow our head and bend our knee in adoration of God.

But humility also means helping others instead of besting others. You know your limits as a human; you understand and are proud of your achievements, but with a strong self-image, you do not always have to win in order to be a person of value. Your worth ironically grows due to your caring service of others. At the Last Supper, Jesus kneels before each of his apostles, and washes their feet, explaining, "I have given you an example that you should do as I have done for you" (John 13:15), adding, "A new command I give you: Love one another. As I have loved you, so you must love one another. By this, all men will know that you are my disciples, if you love one another" (John 13:34–35).

Growth, maturity, and spiritual perfection are, therefore, the degrees to which we love one another— not like, love! We are not to give others the minimum, but the maximum, not only because it is best for others, but also because it is best for us. Serving others does not make you inferior to them. Your worth is due to who you have chosen to be, not simply on what you wear, what you drive, or where you live. Even if you rise to be the richest of the rich, the strongest of the strong, or the smartest of the smart, you are small in contrast to God. And armed with money, strength, and knowledge, you are now able to truly help others. If you hoard your gifts, then you shrink. If you share your gifts, you grow.

This is hard to grasp. Even the apostles argued among themselves as to who was the greatest, being shocked when Jesus told them, "If anyone wants to be first, he must be the very last, and the servant of all" (Mark 9:35), and again, "I tell you the truth, unless you change and become like little children, you will never enter the kingdom of heaven. Therefore, whoever humbles himself like this child is the greatest in the kingdom of heaven" (Matthew 18:3–4).

- *Peace.* A third attribute that you gain is peace. Again, it is misunderstood. Think of going to the Eucharist, at the middle of which we say to one another, "Peace be with you." More often than not, people use it as a time to say hello to friends. However, it is not meant to be a time to catch up with others, but instead to remind one another that we know what life is all about, that Christ rose from the dead, that we shall inherit eternal life, and thus, what do we have to worry about? We are at peace. If someone gave you a present, even a really great one like a car, it is of limited value. Remember your first car? Where is it now? Probably rusting away in a junkyard.

  But the gift of eternal life, ah, that lasts forever. If I told you a secret that would give you another ten years of life free of suffering, I would garnish international fame. But if I told you the secret of eternal life, you might scratch your head in confusion or disbelief, wanting something more concrete. Hard to grasp, but once your inner growth advances to a place of peace, nothing can really bother you anymore, nothing can separate you from the love of Christ and all that he has promised you. Listen to St. Paul, "For I am convinced that neither death nor life, neither angels nor demons, neither the present nor the future, nor any powers, neither height nor depth, nor anything else in all creation, will be able to separate us from the love of God that is in Christ Jesus our Lord" (Romans 8:38–39).

So peace is far more than the absence of war; it is the presence of knowledge, our faith relieving you of anxiety and freeing you from stress.

5. **The Epistles** (Paul, John, James, Peter, and Jude)
    The fifth and last section of the Bible are the epistles, where the message of the Gospels is further developed and understood, and then taken to all nations. While John, James, Peter and Jude wrote some of the epistles, the main person writing is St. Paul. We learn in the Acts of the Apostles, that over three journeys (AD 46–49, 49–52, and 54–57), Paul takes the message to the Galatians, Colossians, and Ephesians in Asia Minor (today's Turkey), to the Philippians, Thessalonians, and Corinthians in Greece, and even to the Romans.

    Paul has always amazed me. While paintings and statues often portray him as tall, dark, and handsome, I was shocked to discover that he was in actuality short, fat, bald and sickly, suffering from either malaria or epilepsy that he referred to as his "thorn of the flesh." Nonetheless, this ordinary little man accomplished extraordinary big feats, traveling on foot to bring the good news of the gospels to one and all.

    His message is the same; love is the purpose of life, for even if you have faith to move mountains, but do not have love, you really have nothing. (1 Corinthians 13:3) This is the famous passage that you hear at weddings, but which was meant not just for a bride and groom, but for all of us. I like it because it also defines what love is.

The Ingredients of Love. As the meaning and power of the spiritual often escapes us (it certainly did the Corinthians), we wondering what rewards we get for being good, let us take a deeper look at some of the ingredients that define love. While Paul did not necessarily

63

mean just for a husband and wife, I shall still use the reference to married love, as it is so common to our experience.

1. *Patient.* Who you get on your wedding day is not who your spouse will be five years from now. Remember, the purpose of marriage is a creative interaction, helping each of you to grow.

    o   Perhaps that means learning to argue with sensitivity instead of aggression, to talk instead of yell, remembering that the goal is intimacy, not victory.

    o   Whatever your goal may be, each of us must be patient with our spouse. As long as they are receptive to the gift of your suggestion, and are making a genuine effort to change, the speed of that change is far less important. Be patient in helping each other with this work of art that we call our maturity. Remember, your spouse will also have to be patient with you!

2. *Kind.* What usually throws people off track in these arguments that bring growth is the way they express their ideas and feelings.

    o   If you come across arrogant and demanding, trying to control and manipulate to turn the other into the person you want, then you get *defensiveness, procrastination, and broken promises.*

    o   While *what* you say may be wonderful, *how* you say it may wash away all the value of your ideas. Assertiveness is defined as not just directly saying what is on your mind, but also saying it with sensitivity. It is not just sandpaper, but also blankets.

    o   Your spouse does not want a teacher or a boss, just a lover.

3. *Not Envious, Not Pretentious.* One of things that marriage can truly help is your insecurity.

o You wake up early on the morning after your wedding, and wonder, "I am so lucky that he or she married me!" You wonder why they did. Are they blind? Can they not see your countless flaws? Or, did they see something inside of you that you often doubt exists? Obviously, it is the latter. They married you because of *who* you are, not because of *what* you have. You can lose your job, and be taking vacations in your backyard instead of Disneyland and still know that you are loved.

o But what if both of you are so insecure that you can't see the forest for the trees, both of you hiding from others because of a fear that you are not as good as they are. Then you will be envious of what others have, or shove in their faces all the symbols of value that you and your spouse could amass.

o You need to remember the pearl of great price, your love for each other. Your spouse married you because of internal qualities that do not fade regardless of the ups and downs of life. You are sensitive, kind, responsible, reliable, considerate, caring, forgiving, humble, and truthful.

o That is what defines your worth, those *internal* qualities that last forever, not the *external* symbols that rust and fade. So don't let the pressures of our materialistic society cloud your vision of what really matters as your love grows.

4. *Bears with all things, hopes all things.* There is no question that we shall trip and fall on our way towards growth in marriage. We shall make mistakes, say insensitive, sarcastic, and cruel things to win arguments or in retaliation for feeling hurt.

o What are you to do? Punish the other, extracting your pound of flesh? No. As I have said before, the punishment for being selfish is to *be* selfish. The punishment for doing dumb things is built right in, your behavior hurting you far more than any revenge from your spouse.

o   So we are asked to forgive, remembering that forgiveness is based less on the premise that the forgiver is kind, and more on the fact that the person being forgiven can change—that they have the potential to do better, to amend their lives, to grow. Love means recognizing that, if your spouse is genuinely sorry, and is honestly trying to change their behavior, then you should forgive them, showing them that you believe in their ability to change and be a better person. You married your spouse for their wonderful qualities. Well, while those qualities may at times be a bit tarnished, they are still there.

o   Once you forgive, you then reap the benefits by having your spouse's new behavior touch your soul, refreshing you as it does him or her.

o   You also up the chance that when you inevitably make a mistake, your spouse will forgive you, instead of being bitter.

Sticking with the theme of marriage for a moment longer, why do you actually go to a wedding? Coming to the wedding ceremony is not a boring prerequisite to be then entitled to all the food and fun that follows at the reception. There are two reasons, each rooted in love.

First, it is a gift for the couple. As this process of growth is difficult, as life has more than a few bumps built into it, you come to offer your support to the couple, to be there for them when they hit a rough time in their marriage.

- Just as they now surround each other in love, you surround them as a couple with your love.
- Just as they are committed to each other, you are committed to them, not out of duty, but out of love.

- The couple will receive a number of gifts from you today, but the main one that will not rust or fade, or end up at the back of a closet, is your love.

But wait, there is also a gift for you. The reason that marriage is a sacrament is that marriage is a sign of how much God loves you. We cannot see God, and hence, we need sacraments or signs to help us see in the material world what we cannot see in the spiritual one.

- If you ever wonder whether God loves you, take a long hard look at the couple. While they are nervous, they also are very much in love.
- God loves you as deeply as that. If you were to stand at the Pearly Gates today and worry if you would gain entry into heaven, and then discovered that your spouse was on the other side and could decide whether or not you get in, you would probably relax instantly, as you know he or she would immediately let you in. Because they love you.
- Well, God loves you that much and more. So when you doubt whether God really cares, look at the couple on the day of their wedding and get a glimpse of the answer, God loves you very, very much.
- So after you take your Pepto-Bismol before going to bed on the night of the wedding, remember the love of the couple as a sacrament or sign of the love that God has for you. All else will fade, but that will endure forever.

Conclusion

So good deeds are rewarded, just not as you thought. The rewards will not be material (long life, lots of kids, lots of land, and lots of possessions), but spiritual (the ability to love deeply and be loved, having an inner contentment and peace, as well as qualities such as patience, kindness, forgiveness, and humility). And those who hurt you will suffer by their lack of that growth, the torment of that emptiness plaguing them not only in this life, but also in the next, eternally. Not sure about life after death? Then turn the page.

7
Is There Life After Death?

Life after death is certainly affirmed in scripture. So let us begin by looking at some of the references about heaven, hell, and *our* resurrection in the Bible.

Heaven

Believers rewarded in heaven

- Matthew 5:12: "Rejoice and be glad, because great is your reward in heaven."
- 1 Peter 1:3–4: "In his great mercy, he has given us a new birth into a living hope through the resurrection of Jesus Christ from the dead, and into an inheritance that can never perish, spoil or fade—kept in heaven for you."

Happiness of heaven

- Revelations 7:16–17: "Never again will they hunger; never again will they thirst. The sun will not beat upon them, nor any scorching heat. For the Lamb at the center of the throne will be their shepherd; he will lead them to springs of living water. And God will wipe away every tear from their eyes."

Lay up treasures in heaven

- Matthew 6:19–20: "Do not store up for yourselves treasures on earth, where moth and rust destroy, and where thieves break in and steal. But store up for yourselves treasure in heaven."
- Luke 12:33: "Do not be afraid, little flock, for your Father has been pleased to give you the kingdom. Sell your possessions and give to the poor. Provide purses for yourselves that will not wear out, a treasure in heaven that will not be exhausted, where no thief comes near and no moth destroys."

Repentance occasions joy in heaven

- Luke 15:7: "I tell you that in the same way there will be more rejoicing in heaven over one sinner who repents than over ninety-nine righteous persons who do not need to repent."

Hell

Destruction from the Presence of God

- 2 Thessalonians 1:8–9: "He will punish those who do not know God and do not obey the gospel of our Lord Jesus. They will be punished with everlasting destruction and shut out from the presence of the Lord and from the majesty of his power."

Soul suffers in hell

- Matthew 10:28: "Do not be afraid of those who kill the body but cannot kill the soul. Rather be afraid of the One who can destroy both soul and body in hell."

Our Resurrection

Believers

- will be glorified with Christ

  o Colossians 3:4: "When Christ, who is your life, appears, then you will also appear with him in glory."

- will have bodies like Christ

  o Philippians 3:21: "the Lord Jesus Christ, who by the power that enables him to bring everything under his control, will transform our lowly bodies so that they will be like his glorious body."
  o 1 John 3:2: "But we know that when he appears, we shall be like him."
  o 1 Corinthians 15:42–44: "So will it be with the resurrection of the dead. The body that is sown perishable, it is raised imperishable; it is sown in dishonor, it is raised in glory; it is sown in weakness, it is raised in power; it is sown a natural body, it is raised a spiritual body."

- will rise through Christ

  o John 11:25: "I am the resurrection and the life. He who believes in me will live, even though he dies;"
  o Acts 4:2: "They (the priests and the Sadducees) were greatly disturbed because the apostles were teaching the people and proclaiming in Jesus the resurrection of the dead."
  o 1 Corinthians 15:21–22: "For since death came through a man, the resurrection of the dead comes also through a man. For as in Adam all die, so in Christ all will be made alive."

- will rise to eternal life

  - o John 5:24, 28–29: "I tell you the truth, who hears my word and believes him who sent me has eternal life and will not be condemned; he has crossed over from death to life."
  - o John 5:28–29: "Do not be amazed at this, for a time is coming when all who are in their graves will hear his voice and come out—those who have done good will rise to live, and those who have done evil will rise to be condemned."
  - o John 6:40: "For my Father's will is that everyone who looks to the Son and believes in him shall have eternal life, and I will raise him up at the last day."

- should look forward to heaven

  - o 2 Corinthians 5:1: "Now we know that if the earthly tent we live in is destroyed, we have a building from God, an eternal house in heaven, not built by humans' hands."
  - o Philippians 3:10–11: "I want to know Christ and the power of his resurrection and the fellowship of sharing in his suffering, becoming like him in his death, and so, somehow, to attain the resurrection of the dead."

How is life after death possible?

- Romans 8:11: "And if the Spirit of him who raised Jesus from the dead is living in you, he who raised Christ from the dead will also give life to your mortal bodies though his Spirit, who lives in you."
- 2 Corinthians 5:5: "Now it is God who has made us for this very purpose and has given us the Spirit as a deposit, guaranteeing what is to come."

Called in question by some in the primitive church

- 1 Corinthians 15:12: "But if it is preached that Christ has been raised from the dead, how can some of you say that there is no resurrection of the dead?"

Doctrine of the Old Testament

- Job 19:25–27: "I know that my Redeemer lives, and that in the end he will stand upon the earth. And after my skin has been destroyed, yet in my flesh I shall see God. I myself will see him with my own eyes—I, and not another. How my heart yearns within me!"
- Psalm 16:10: "because you will not abandon me to the grave, nor will you let your faithful one see decay."
- Psalm 49:15: "But God will redeem my life from the grave; he will surely take me to himself."
- Isaiah 26:19: "But your dead will live; their bodies will rise. You who dwell in the dust, wake up and shout for joy. Your dew is like the dew of the morning; the earth will give birth to her dead."
- Daniel 12:2: "Multitudes who sleep in the dust of the earth will awake; some to everlasting life, others to shame and everlasting contempt."
- Hosea 13:14: "I will ransom them from the power of the grave; I will redeem them from death. Where, O death, are your plagues? Where, O grave, is your destruction?"

Argument for Life After Death

Desire to Be Perfectly Happy

Even with all those scriptural references, people still have doubts. Admittedly, it is difficult to prove something that is spiritual by material facts.

But how about logic? If God exists, what then can be said about him? Earlier we have deduced that he must be eternal vs. temporal, omnipresent vs. limited in space, omnipotent vs. limited in power, and omniscient vs. limited in knowledge.

Well, here is another thought. If God created that which is good, then does it not make sense that he too is good? Theologians tell us that God is love and that God is the quintessence of goodness.

Humans have a universal desire to be perfectly happy. Yet no one is. If God is good, would he then deny us the one thing that we all crave? If so, God would be cruel, implanting in us the desire for perfect happiness, and then dangling it in front of us knowing that we cannot attain it. It would be like someone dangling a steak in front of a hungry dog. That would make God evil. But God is the quintessence of goodness, and so there is no evil in him. Consequently, if we all desire to be perfectly happy, but that perfect happiness is not possible on earth, is it not logical that God would make it possible somewhere else? That somewhere else we call heaven.

What is Perfect Happiness?

But as there is a hell, some people obviously do not receive perfect happiness. Why?

Well, what is perfect happiness? It is not primarily a healthy body, but a healthy soul; after all, a human is made up of both body and soul. If our purpose in life is to learn how to love, and if that is determined by the choices that we daily make by our own free will, then that leaves the door open for some to choose wisely and some not.

I can befriend you or manipulate you. I can choose to be kind to you or cruel. I can choose to cooperate with you or to control you. I can view you as a sucker of whom I can take advantage, or as a potential friend whom I can get to know and, when needed, help.

Think for a minute of the people whom you have met during your life. Upon having conversations with them, you learn of their character. If you encounter someone who is not nice, you may be brave enough to lovingly confront him or her, hoping to help him or her choose a different direction. However, if they consistently refuse, you then may choose not to spend time with them, as they only care about themselves. They are not trying to grow with you; they are trying to use you. They are sucking you dry. You do not back away due to any ill will for that person, but because they are hurting you and it is all right to take good care of yourself, separating yourself from those who can be toxic.

Now, imagine that person goes through life following the same path. They have become increasingly cynical, sarcastic, selfish, and without true friends. They have no healthy relationships, and they impress you as sad. Yet it was their choice. Others like you have tried to help them, have tried to give them the opportunity for change and growth, but they have consistently pushed you and others away, contemptuously wondering what you want from them.

Hell is not a place. It is a state of mind. Living an eternal life without real friends, being alone and bitter, while simultaneously seeing others having a wonderful time, that is hell.

While there is an afterlife, it seems logical that we all go to the same place. However, how we live in that place is determined by how we chose to live in this place, earth. Hell, therefore, is not fire and brimstone, but spiritual emptiness.

Yes, in the states of mind called heaven and hell, we all shall have new bodies that do not decay or age, being in perfect health for all eternity. However, a healthy body and a sad soul make for hell, whereas a healthy body and a happy soul make for heaven. Heaven is where you are in loving and constant contact with all whom you love: your spouse, your parents, your children, your grandchildren, your friends, and, of course, God.

Heaven or hell are the results of your choices on earth, your growth ending in death, and God simply allowing you to have what you chose over and over again with your own freewill.

Some might say that is unfair, that we deserve another chance. But we have had many, many chances throughout our lives.

Consider the story of the rich man and the beggar (Luke 17:19–31). The rich man is dressed in the finest of clothes and lives in luxury. Outside is a beggar named Lazarus, whom the rich man never helps. They both die at the same time. The rich man wakes up to see the poor man far above him with Abraham, and cries out for help. However, he is told by Abraham, "Son, remember that in your lifetime you received your good things, while Lazarus received bad things, but now he is comforted here and you are in agony. And besides all this, between us and you a great chasm has been fixed, so that those who want to go from here to you cannot, nor can anyone cross over from there to us." Sensing how his bad choices during life have condemned him to a life in hell, he asks that word be sent to his brothers to warn them. But Abraham tells him, "If they do not listen to Moses and the Prophets, they will not be convinced even if someone rises from the dead." Bottom line, they have had many chances, and a lot of help in making their choices in life. If they choose to ignore all of those signs, then the consequences of their choices will fall on their heads just as they have on the rich man.

God, therefore, holds our feet to the fire regarding the consequences that we have freely chosen. You had a lifetime to change. Death is the end of that process, which is why hanging over our earthly heads is the thought "carpe diem (seize the day)," for it will not come again.

What If You Die Young?

If life is a process of growth through the choices we make, what if life is cut short? What if you die young? How unfair is that!

That always puzzled me. When I was ordained only a year, I was called to the house of parents whose baby was dying of brain cancer. They were so upset that their child would be robbed of a normal life. Would their son be stuck with the growth of an infant? Would he be cheated out of a lifetime of growth? How could that make any sense?

Then one year, the meaning of a parable that I had read over and over again hit me like a ton of bricks. It is the *Parable of the Workers in the Vineyard* (Matthew 20:1–16).

It is the story of different people going to work in a vineyard at different times during the day. Some begin early in the morning, others start later, at the third, sixth, ninth, and eleventh hours of the day. At the end of the day, they all line up to be paid. When those who worked a full day see that the one who had only worked one hour getting paid for a full day, they grumble, complaining that it is unfair to them. The owner tells them that he promised a full day's wage for a full day's work. They got what he promised. If he wants to be kind and generous to the guy who only worked an hour, who are they to complain.

I have to admit that for years, I was rather dense, agreeing with those who complained. Then, it dawned on me that the parable is not talking about work, but life. It means that, if we die too soon through no fault of our own, God, being generous, gives us the full measure of growth that we would have attained if we lived a full life.

So that baby was given the full measure of happiness and maturity that he would have had should he have lived to be an old man. Wow!

Then it made sense to me why the saints of old were so bold and courageous. If they were arrested and executed for their faith, the growth that would have been theirs had they lived a long life was given to them. The fear of death had no power over them.

Thus, the fear of death should have no power over us either. We cannot be cheated or robbed out of the growth that we deserve. We certainly do not wish to die too soon, but should a car accident, a stroke, or a heart attack end our lives too early, there is nothing to fear. Jesus tells us not to worry, that if God clothes the lilies of the field who neither labor or spin, he will certainly take care of us (Matthew 6:28–30). So let this soothe your anxiety and give you a deep sense of peace.

Theological Basis for Belief in Life After Death

But how is it possible that we who are temporal can have hope of an eternal life after this one?

Think for a minute about Christmas. When God became man, man was metaphysically linked to God. When Jesus, the Son of God, entered humanity through the willingness of Mary by his birth in Bethlehem, the Holy Spirit, who is eternal, flowed into humanity, not from the birth of Christ onwards, but also backwards to the beginning of time, for Jesus was not only man, but also God, not only in time, but also eternity.

As Christians, we believe that we have the Holy Spirit within each of us. Do you remember being told as a child that your body was a temple of the Holy Spirit? It is the dwelling of the Holy Spirit within us that enables us to pass from this life to the next. Consider again these scriptural passages:

- Romans 8:11: "And if the Spirit of him who raised Jesus from the dead is living in you, he who raised Christ from the dead will also give life to your mortal bodies though his Spirit, who lives in you."
- 2 Corinthians 5:5: "Now it is God who has made us for this very purpose and has given us the Spirit as a deposit, guaranteeing what is to come."

So our body dies, but our spirit goes through the door from earth to heaven instantly. When our families are crying upon learning of our death, we are having the best day ever—dwarfing any day we had on earth. The last breath we shall take on earth will be followed by the first breath we take in heaven. God does not condemn us to someplace called purgatory or limbo, but instead immediately carries us through his eternal spirit to a new life, a life with a new body and a soul that must now live the life that was chosen by all the decisions we made each day of our lives.

The judgment of God is to accept our judgment. God is not whimsical in his decision. He merely forces you to live as you have freely chosen to live, a little or a lot due to having chosen a path of love or of emptiness. There are many degrees to our union with God. All of us, whether we are good or bad, have the Holy Spirit dwelling within us, and so pass from this life to the next. However, the degree of our growth, the degree to which we have grown to be like Christ, which is due to our choices on earth, defines the degree of our happiness in heaven.

Reflect upon your receiving communion at church. We physically eat the body of Christ and drink his blood. Just as the food you eat becomes part of you, so too do you commune with Christ by receiving the bread and wine.

But we also are told to spiritually become more like him; that Jesus is the way to the Father. While hard to understand (certainly Thomas and Philip did not get it), Jesus tried to be blunt, saying, "I am the way, and the truth, and the life" (John 14:6–7), meaning as to the degree that we are like Christ, to that same degree do we commune with God. It is not complicated, Jesus having made it exceedingly simple when saying, "A new command I give you: Love one another. As I have loved you, so you must love one another. By this all men will know that you are my disciples, if you love one another" (John 13:34–35). Loving is easy to understand, but hard to do, but we have a lifetime of "doing" to gradually grow in love.

So that you go to a life after death is a gift of God through his Spirit. How you go to that life is a gift you give yourself by how you commune with Christ in our love of one another, being determined by a lifetime of choices that fashion the person whom you will be for eternity.

Near-Death Experiences

A final thought to ponder is the reality of near-death experiences that attest to visions of heaven. John Burke, the pastor of the Gateway Church in Austin, Texas, wrote a fascinating book entitled, *Imagine Heaven: Near-Death Experiences. God's Promises, and the Exhilarating Future that Awaits You* (Grand Rapids, Michigan: Baker Books, 2015).

While some sneer and cast aspersions on such experiences, it is interesting that they have a commonality, and that having experienced a near death, the person affected is convinced of life after death.

John Burke describing himself as "a former skeptic," reports about some of the one thousand near-death stories of which he had heard over thirty-five years. He reported that, while the interpretations of these events varied, "the shared core experience points to what Scripture says" (p. 15). When speaking of his book, he writes, "If nothing else, it will open your eyes to the millions of accounts out there that have convinced skeptical doctors, atheistic college professors, and many others (all of whose stories you will read) that Heaven is real" (p. 17).

Conclusion

So is there life after death? Scriptures tell us that there is. Jesus tells us that there is. Logic tells us that there is. And near-death experiences tell us that there is. Does that resolve all your doubts? No, but it certainly narrows the gap between what we can prove and what we must believe.

8

How Do You Deal with Depression and Self-Doubt?

While the issue of depression is psychological, it can certainly derail your spiritual journey. Hence, I want to help you get over that obstacle.

Definition

What is depression? It has numerous definitions, such as anger turned in, or, the one I like is that depression is a gap between *who you are* (the ego) and *who you think you should be* (the ego ideal). If you cannot attain who you think you should be, then you fall into the chasm in between the ego and ego ideal called depression. You think that you do not measure up, that you are a failure, and that you might as well stop trying.

Dynamics

How did this begin? Well, who we think we should be is largely determined by our parents. They encourage us to attain goals, such as to walk, to potty train, to eat our vegetables, to tell the truth, to get good grades in school, to participate in sports, and so on. However, if they somehow convey that our worth is predicated upon the achievement of those goals, then the formula of depression takes root. We think that our self-worth is due to getting an A in spelling, getting a hit in baseball, getting into the right college, marrying the right person, getting a good job, getting promotions, and so on.

When we are children, this can be reinforced by being told that we are a "good boy" or "good girl," or that we have let them down when we do not perform as our parents had hoped. Wanting to please our parents, we run faster and faster, trying to reach the goals that will make them happy, decreasing their criticism and increasing their praise. But as you can see, our worth then is predicated not upon who we are, but upon what we do, and even if we succeed, we feel like a mouse on a treadmill condemned to always perform and reach higher and higher goals.

At some point, this dynamic becomes deeply internalized, and so we no longer connect our depressed mood to our parents, but now to someone to whom we have transferred that power: a teacher, a spouse, a boss, or anyone whose praise we seek. While the person whom we wish to please changes, what remains the same is that our self-worth comes from outside of ourselves.

Healing

The solution, and what therapy involves, is to help a depressed person determine their worth from within instead of without of themselves. This does not mean candy coating reality, but quite the opposite. We need to take a long hard look at ourselves. We can look at those areas that need improvement, but we also need to see that our positives far outweigh our negatives. It is only when we take back the power to determine our own worth that depression can be conquered.

Our worth should not be conditional upon our performance, but upon our inner self. As far as self-worth is concerned, the arrow points not from what we do to who we are, but from who we are to what we do. Think about it. What you have achieved is due to you. You have a mind to think, a will to love, and fine qualities such as sensitivity, caring, truthfulness, responsibility, reliability, prudence, and thoughtfulness. Without that inner core of strength, nothing could be accomplished.

Depression puts the cart in front of the horse, erroneously defining you by what you do instead of by who you are. Healing is putting you in front of not only what you do, but also in front of what anybody else thinks of you. Having done so, you can still be hurt by what others may say, but you will not be devastated. It is as if you have a psychological suit of armor on that cannot be pierced by the slings and arrows of others.

And why would you give others so much power? A secret that I have learned in life is that everyone feels insecure. The most secure admit it, but the least secure deny it, hiding behind a mask of superiority. They can be so good at it that we think that they have it all together, and we must keep struggling to hopefully one day be like them. But that condemns you to a life of being depressed, for even if someone gives you the praise you want, the good feeling soon wears out, and so you again struggle to get the other person to either repeat or increase the adulation you so desperately seek.

So therapy is not helping you to attain what others think you should be (the ego ideal), but to throw that away and come to love and accept who you are (the ego). Whatever mask you may have put on to fool others is of far less value than the person hiding underneath—you.

Patience

While this may sound easy, it is not. Even if you understand and agree with what I am saying, realize that your tendency to define yourself by what you do and what others think of you is deeply ingrained. Hence, you will be shocked to find that the new you is still vulnerable to the criticism of others, often plunging you into a deep and dark mood. But now you have the key to unlock that prison cell, freeing you from what others think to the reality of who you are. So do not think that you have somehow failed therapy. No, you have been armed with the solution that you must apply over and over again until your down moods become less prevalent and less severe.

Medication

Of course, therapy is good, but not enough. Medication is also important. Why? Because when you become depressed, there is a decrease in the brain of what are called neurotransmitters, such as serotonin. Whereas when you are happier, your mind could easily dispel negative thoughts, when you are depressed, your brain cells are firing so sluggishly that your mind gets trapped in the web of your negative thoughts. You may have heard of the saying, "think happy, be happy." An antidepressant does not "make" you happy, but increases the number of neurotransmitters so that you can think more clearly, to more accurately see the truth of who you are—a work of art.

Final Thoughts

Well, I hope this bridge that I built for you will help you cross over from confusion to understanding, from what you can prove to what you choose to believe, and from discouragement to hope.

I meant that the book would be short, so that more people would be encouraged to read it instead of feeling overwhelmed by a huge tome in front of them. While what I have written summarizes my own personal journey, I am still travelling deeper and deeper into understanding life, becoming more like Christ, and thus becoming a happier person. While our bodily growth stops when we reach a certain height, our spiritual growth continues until we take our last breath.

Hence, what I have written is not the end point of my journey, just a look back at where I have been. As my journey has been difficult, I have built this bridge to make yours easier.

Going forward, for me each day offers the opportunity to continue deepening my understanding. Each time I work to prepare a sermon for a church I shall help on a Sunday, my hours of study are like eating candy. I gain a little more spiritual clarity into life, even if my physical eyesight wanes in clarity. While I could be discouraged by the latter, I choose to be excited by the former. After all, the physical will eventually die, but the spiritual will live forever.

So on your journey, do not be penny-wise and pound-foolish. Put your effort into what will last, that is, who you choose to be by how you relate to others. After all, you are worth it!

References

Barton, John, and John Muddiman. 2001. Eds., *The Oxford Bible Commentary*. New York: Oxford University Press.

Brown, Raymond E., Joseph A. Fitzmyer, and Roland E. Murphy, Eds. 1968. *The Jerome Biblical Commentary*. Englewood Cliffs, New Jersey: Prentice-Hall, Inc.

Burke, John. 2015. *Imagine Heaven: Near-Death Experiences. God's Promises, and the Exhilarating Future That Awaits You*. Grand Rapids, Michigan: Baker Books.

Collins, Francis S. 2006. *The Language of God: A Scientist Presents Evidence for Belief*. New York: Free Press.

Kushner, Harold S. 1981. *When Bad Things Happen to Good People*. New York: Anchor Books.

McKenzie, John L. 1965. *Dictionary of the Bible*. Milwaukee: The Bruce Publishing Company.

Pegis, Anton C., Ed. 1945. *Basic Writings of Saint Thomas Aquinas*, 1. New York: Random House.

Stimpson, Peter K. 2008. *Map to Happiness: Straightforward Advice on Everyday Issues*. Lincoln, Nebraska: iUniverse.

Zacharias, Ravi and Vince Vitale. 2017. *Jesus Among Secular Gods: The Countercultural Claims of Christ*. New York: Faith Words.

About the Author

Peter K. Stimpson is an Episcopal priest and a licensed clinical social worker. He has counseled people from all walks of life since 1972 and retired in 2014 as director of Trinity Counseling Service in Princeton, New Jersey.

His first book, *Map to Happiness: Straightforward Advice on Everyday Issues,* was published in 2008. Reverend Stimpson also wrote a popular advice column in various newspapers from 1983–2014.

Reverend Stimpson holds master's degrees from the University of Ottawa in theology and from the State University of New York at Albany in social work.

CPSIA information can be obtained
at www.ICGtesting.com
Printed in the USA
LVHW031439120319
610369LV00002B/320/P